The History of Nature

The
History
of
Nature

By C. F. von WEIZSÄCKER

THE UNIVERSITY OF CHICAGO PRESS

First published in German under the title DIE GESCHICHTE DER NATUR by S. Hirzel Verlag, Zürich, Switzerland. Translated by Fred D. Wieck.

H

THE UNIVERSITY OF CHICAGO PRESS, CHICAGO 37
Cambridge University Press, London, N.W. 1, England
W. J. Gage & Co., Limited, Toronto 2B, Canada

Table of Contents

I

Introduction

MY SUBJECT is the history of nature. This means that I have set myself a theme far broader than is the custom in the run of academic writing. No scientist can master all the fields of knowledge touched upon in an essay of this sort. Therefore, I should perhaps begin with an attempt to justify my choice of subject.

We are becoming more and more aware of the danger that lies in the specialization of the sciences. We are vexed by the barriers that are raised to separate the various disciplines from one another. Specialized science is powerless to give us a world-view that could sustain us in the confusion of our existence. And so we are longing for synthesis, searching for the point of vantage from which to gain perspective.

But if we are to overcome the errors that lie in the self-limitation of the several disciplines, we must first of all understand what in this self-limitation is justified. Specialization does not spring from accident, or from a whimsy of the scientists, but is a fateful consequence of the very character of science. A man's fate is most often shaped by that trait of his character which contains at once both the possibility of his greatest virtue, and the temptation to his

greatest vice. In the true scientist, this determining character trait is his awareness of his intellectual responsibility
for the particular. Others may sense, believe, profess—the
scientist inquires. He believes only the results that he has
gained from inquiry. He believes only where he knows.
Now it is impossible to know all one would like to know,
or even all one ought to know. It follows that the scientific attitude always means a resignation and a self-denial—
even for the most fertile scientist. This self-denial is the
source of specialization. Like any sacrifice made in full
awareness, it may deserve our admiration, when it is due
to the feeling of responsibility. Or it may deserve our contempt, when it is due merely to the lack of effort for
perspective. In any case, it has become the fate of science.

The those of our characteristics that become our fate are
seldom wholly independent of our will. If we want to
counteract specialization, what is there in the scientist's
nature and mind to which we might appeal?

The scientist is never only a scientist. He is at the same
time a living human being, he is a member of mankind.
And so, his responsibility for the particular is counter-
balanced by his share of responsibility for the whole. He
has to ask himself: What is the meaning of my inquiry for
the lives of my fellows?—Can I answer for the effects that
my work has upon the life of mankind?

The effect of science upon life is summed up in a well-
known saying: Knowledge is Power. We will have to
admit this truth today even if until recently we may have
been inclined to doubt it. But, is power good? Man has
learned to build the instruments of power. Will he learn
to master them?

Some people are convinced that man will never learn this mastery, and so they believe that we ought to renounce a science that places such instruments of power in our hands. I can hardly presume all by myself to settle this problem once and for all. But it is my feeling that what is proposed here as a solution is something that is impossible. I believe that our world cannot in fact give up the knowledge that is the source of power. This or that individual man may give it up, but the world in general will not give it up. And if this is true, then is not the man who does give up science, dodging perhaps the responsibility he should help to bear?

But how can he bear the responsibility?

If knowledge and the power that comes from knowledge can be good at all, they can be so only in the hands of good men. The choices that must here be made do not lie in the sphere of science but in that of morals. I would add as my personal conviction that they do not even lie solely in the sphere of morals, but in that of religion. It is not my task here to discuss the practical aspects of the choices. But I believe I must point out that they are unavoidable. And it is my task, I believe, to raise the question what our science must be like if we as scientists want to shoulder our share of responsibility for the whole.

Power is only one side of knowledge. The other side I would call insight—an inadequate term, I admit. The knowledge that brings power is instrumental knowledge. It asks, what ends can I accomplish with the given means?, what means do I require to bring about a desired end? The human motives that prompt me to desire a specific end are not considered. Man in this context appears as a completely free and irresponsible being. He is the subject who as master confronts an object in no way akin to him. Instrumental knowledge is knowledge of fragments, and is content with that. It can be satisfied with a science that is completely specialized. Insight, on the other hand, I would call that knowledge which considers the coherence of the whole. Insight must be especially concerned with man himself, his motives and his aims, and with the inner and outer conditions of his existence. Insight may not separate subject and object fundamentally, but must recognize their essential kinship, their mutual dependence and, consequently, their inseparable coherence.

Let me be quite clear: I do not think that such insight constitutes in itself a cure for our age. Every insight can be abused by an ill will, even by a merely misdirected will. But those among us who in this instrumentalized world of ours want to work for the good will search for insight. They will search for the coherence within which the instruments have their origin and their potential meaning. Not that insight produces the decision for what is good, but this decision, once it is made, desires insight.

As we are trying to achieve such insight, the notion of responsibility for the whole acquires a specific, concrete meaning. It now means the responsibility for the whole which is the totality of all sciences, the *universitas literarum*. For insight in this sense clearly is to be found, not in the several disciplines but only in their interconnection, not in the single bricks but only in the whole edifice of the sciences. It is in this sense that the present chapter is concerned with the totality of science.

Is this totality real? Is it not an empty dream?

The deepest rift that is at present dividing the edifice of science is the cleavage between natural science and the humanistic disciplines. Natural science, by means of instrumental thinking, inquires into the material world around us. The humanistic disciplines study man, and they accept him such as man knows himself: as soul, consciousness, mind. The cleavage resides not so much in the subject matter—that overlaps in part—as in approach and method. Natural science is founded on the sharp distinction of the comprehending subject from the object which is comprehended. To the humanistic disciplines falls the much harder task of turning even the subject, in his subjectivity, into an object of their understanding. Many an attempted conversation shows that these two modes of thought understand each other only very rarely. But it seems to me that, beyond this mutual misunderstanding, there lies in readiness the possibility of an objective connection between both groups of disciplines, waiting only to be seen and to be made a reality. Let me indicate this connection by a simile: Natural science and humanistic disciplines appear to me like two half-circles. They ought to be joined in such a way that they combine to form a full circle, and this circle ought then to be followed round fully, many times. By this I mean:

On the one hand, man is himself a being of nature. Nature is older than man. Man has come out of nature and is subject to her laws. An entire science, medical science, is successfully engaged in studying man as a part of nature, with the methods of natural science. In this sense, the humanistic disciplines presuppose natural science.

On the other hand, natural science is itself made by man

and for man, and is subject to the conditions of every intellectual and material work of man. Man is older than natural science. Nature had to be so that there could be man—man had to be so that there could be concepts of nature. It is possible as well as necessary to understand natural science as a part of man's intellectual life. In this sense, natural science presupposes the humanistic disciplines.

Both groups of disciplines see as a rule only one side of this mutual dependence. The thinking in the circle of mutual dependence may even awaken the suspicion that we are thinking in a vicious circle where A is proved by B and B in turn by A. But we are dealing here not with logical deductions but with the dependence of real things on one another, and they often close in a circle. Conceptual thinking has split the original unity of man and nature into the opposition of subject and object. The circle of which I am speaking is meant as the first, though perhaps not the last step in a direction which should once again make the unity of the two opposites accessible to our thinking. Only when we understand clearly and in detail the dependence of man upon nature, and of the concepts of nature upon man, only when we have rounded the circle many times, only then, at best, may we hope to see reality as one, science as a whole.

I am not aiming in this chapter at so comprehensive an achievement. Excepting a few digressions, I shall speak only of one of the half-circles—of nature, and man's origin in nature. But in return, I mean to speak of the whole of nature, as far as that is possible in such limited space. Again, this cannot be done in all fullness but only under one specific aspect. The aspect I have chosen is the historic side of nature. Of course, I have made this choice so as to keep before our eyes the connection with the humanistic disciplines. For one of the most important of humanistic disciplines is the one called history.

Among the fundamental convictions of many humanists is that man and man alone is a historic being. To this conviction I would oppose the assertion: Man is indeed a historic being, but this is possible because man comes out of nature and because nature is historic herself. What distinguishes man is not that he has a history, but that he has an understanding of his history. Here I must first explain the sense in which I am using the concept "history." In doing so I shall at the same time explain the purpose of the present chapter.

History is what happens. Yet it includes not only what happens now, but also what has happened and what will happen. History occurs in the past, the present, and the future—for short, in time. History in the broadest sense is the essence of what happens in time. In this sense, nature undoubtedly has a history since nature herself is in time. History of nature, then, would be the totality of what happens in nature.

But the humanistic disciplines and philosophy, particularly in recent times, have become accustomed to a narrower concept of history. We shall arrive at this narrower concept by a gradual refinement of the concept with which we have started.

History is only where there is change. In pride or in agony, mankind experiences the turmoil of its history—eternally unmoved, without history, the starred heavens look on. A stone that sleeps beneath the ground millions of years has no history—above it, historic life blooms and withers, hurries and grows.

History is only where there is irrevocable change. The planets revolve even in the skies, but since billions of years their paths have been forever the same. The planetary system is in constant motion, but fundamentally it does not change. Hence it is without history. The same seems to hold true of living nature. Every spring anew the woods cover themselves with leaves, and every fall they turn bare again. They are a symbol for us of the unchanging cycle of history-less nature. But man experiences events that separate past and present irrevocably. In himself alone, not in nature, does man undergo the basic experience of the historic: we do not step twice into the same river.

But nature's appearance of being without history is an illusion. All depends on the time scale we use. To the mayfly whose life spans one day, man is without history; to man, the forest; to the forest, the stars; but to a being who has learned to contain within his mind the idea of eternity, even the stars are historic essences. A hundred years ago none of us was alive. Twenty thousand years ago the forest did not stand, and our country was covered with ice. A billion years ago the limestone that I find in the ground today did not yet exist. Ten billion years ago, there was most likely neither sun nor earth nor any of the stars we know. There is a theorem of physics, the Second Law of thermodynamics, according to which events in nature are fundamentally irreversible and incapable of repetition. This law I should like to call the law of the historic character of nature. In the fourth chapter it will be discussed at length.

However, there is indeed a fundamental difference between man and nature. Nature undergoes history, but she does not experience it. She is history but does not have history, because she does not know that she is history. And why does man alone have a conscious, experienced history? Because he alone has consciousness and experience. And so it does seem to me meaningful after all to see man's distinction not in his historic existence as such, but in his awareness of his historic existence. True, the historic existence of a conscious being is likely to differ from that of a non-conscious being. And as we study in what manner man has a history, we shall add to our knowledge of history in general, and to our knowledge of the history of nature.

At this point the concept of time needs closer study.

Time is the past, the present, and the future. What is the meaning of these three mysterious words?

Let us first consider a notion of time that disregards the differences between past, present, and future. The astronomer who studies the motion of the planets, or the physicist who studies the waning oscillations of a pendulum, treat time as little else than a fourth coordinate beside the three coordinates of space. This spatialization of time finds its most striking symbol in the graphic time schedule of the railroader. This schedule shows on one coordinate the distance the train travels, on the other coordinate the length of time in which the train covers the distance. Which portion of the train's course is past, which future, and where the present moment lies—that is irrelevant in the nature of the schedule. The schedule is not concerned with the question whether the train already has run according to it, or will run according to it in the future.

This concept of time, however, is an abstraction. You and I are concerned whether the train runs on schedule, and there is then a decisive difference between past and future. It can be known whether or not the train has in the past run on schedule. That is an unalterable fact. But whether the train will run on schedule in the future, that cannot be known with certainty, not even in the best of all railroad systems. It is possible, it is to be hoped, it is likely—but it is not a fact, until it has become a present and then, quickly, a past event. Past and future events have different modes of being: past events are factual, future events possible. Neither are real in the strictest sense; actually real is only the present. But both past and future events are of the greatest significance for us. The past has created the framework of facts in which our present is held inescapably. History is fate. And the future will at one time be the present, so that we have a vital interest in it. We attempt to penetrate the future, to guide it. We constantly anticipate future events in our imagination. Our imagination treats that which is possible as if it were already actual. And indeed, at one time it will be actual.

This structure of time is what I want to call from here on its historic character. It has no analogies in space, or only very imperfect ones. It follows that the spatialization of time of which I have spoken is doing violence to the phenomenon "time." And this holds true not only for time as man experiences it, but also for the concept of time that we have to have in order to give an adequate description of nature. Perhaps I can explain this best by offering my defense against a counter-assertion that the pure natural scientists might easily throw up to me in reproach, and that might run like this: Everything that happens is in reality predetermined. That we do not know it is merely a sign of our human frailty. Man is only a small part of nature, and if we want to define so basic a concept as time, we must not introduce into the definition the limitations of our human understanding, but must transcend them.

This objection might first of all be countered with the question: Why is it, then, that the future is hidden from us so much more completely than the past? However, our methodical inquiry must search deeper, and we must now remember the full circle whose two halves are natural science and the humanistic disciplines. The tendency to blur the distinction between past and future by calling the future completely predetermined, is a characteristic of natural science. Natural science itself, however, is a specific product of the human mind, and the question that we must raise is, what does this tendency of natural science signify for the life of man.

After all, we know nature only through the medium of human experience. As concerns man, now, the past certainly is that which is factual and largely known, the future that which is merely possible and unknown. We have a memory for the past, but no corresponding faculty for the future. Still, even the future is not wholly inaccessible, and all our scheming and planning is intent on knowing something of the future beforehand. One of the means to gain foreknowledge is natural science. I have called its thinking instrumental. This means precisely that natural science strives to gain such knowledge as will allow us to know the future beforehand and perhaps even to influence it. The conceptual tool that natural science uses for this task is causal thinking. In many instances we find a strict connection of cause and effect that can be refined into the formulation of a precise mathematical relation between the states of things at different moments in time. Now the future can in part be calculated—in part, that is, as far as our chains of causes and effects will reach. The spatial representation of time I mentioned belongs in this world of a calculable future. Spatialization of time ends where future events cease being calculable by the law of causality. The technical tool of spatialization is, of course, the clock. On its dial we read elapsing spans of time as spatial lengths. But the clock is a mechanical apparatus. It "runs" only as long as the causal connections in its movement take place without disturbance.

Now the assertion is made that there is "in reality" no essential difference between past and future, since the future as such is likewise strictly determined. But this assertion presupposes that, if only we had a sufficient knowledge of nature, we should be able to give a description of nature in terms of cause and effect, down to the last detail. This is a hypothesis. It may even be a true hypothesis. I shall abstain from discussing here the reasons against determinism that have come to light in atomic physics. I only want to point out that determinism is not a matter of experience. The future as such may be determined, but to us it is not given as determined, neither our own future nor that even of inanimate nature. Immediate intuition, without reference to the question of determinism, shows us the following differences between past and future:

We cannot escape from the moment that is *now*. Every present becomes a past, every future at one time a present. The past, as the essence of facts that once were present, is determined. This determination has nothing to do with causal determination. For the strict chain of causation, starting within the present, does not enable us to compute an unknown past any more than it allows us to compute an unknown future. Basically, both the past and the future eclipses of the sun are equally easy or difficult of computation. Those in the past, however, have surely taken place, while those in the future can be predicted only with that degree of certainty with which we would dare to assert that no cosmic catastrophes will intervene. We know that man has existed three thousand years ago, the earth two billion years ago. Would we dare to predict anything whatsoever for an equally distant future? Tomorrow all of us may die from a cause that is still unknown today— no power on earth can change that we were alive yesterday. In later chapters I shall show that the two fundamental principles of the historic character of both animate and inanimate nature—the Second Law, and the tendency toward the evolution of differentiated forms—can be derived from the difference between past and future that I have described, and a few simple assumptions in addition. And that will establish in turn that some of the central theses of natural science can be understood, not by overcoming the historic character of time but only by recognizing it.

To sum up: The past is what at one time was the present. It is made up of factual, unalterable events. The future is what at one time will be the present. It contains possible events, events on which we can exert an influence. Nature is historic insofar as her events take place objectively within the time that is defined as historic by these facts. Man is historic further in that he experiences subjectively the historic character of time, and acts in the manner in which a conscious being has to act in his position: determined by the past, reaching ahead into the future with his cares and his plans.

It follows from the historic character of time that a science of history exists only for the past. Historical science is concerned with telling what has in fact happened, regardless at first whether or not it had to happen. The future, to a certain extent, can be construed hypothetically in advance, and only its transformation into the present will show if the construction was correct. But the past can be studied without such construction, for it consists of facts that have occurred, whether we know them or not.

II

Return into the History of the Earth

LET us go back together, step by step, from where we of the present time are standing, back into the most distant past we have learned to know. From there we shall in turn follow the development of our world, step by step, until we have in our minds rebuilt the ground on which we stand today, and from which we started out.

This chapter falls into three parts. First I shall discuss how it is possible to know anything about the past at all, next the question how an absolute chronology is established for the events in the history of the earth. And finally, I shall attempt to give my reader an idea of the events that have taken place in the various periods of time our methods have established.

What is past is no more, and does not return. How can we know at all something that is past?

The past is immediately present to me in my memory. Memory means that I have "kept in mind" something that has happened, and know it as something that has happened beyond the possibility of a doubt. This is the only form in which I have immediate contact with the past. All other approaches to the past have in them an element of in-directness.

My memory is linked up with the conditions of my ex-istence. I remember only what I have experienced myself. We need not dwell on the fact that I may forget even that. It is clear that the place and the time of my experience fix the external limits of what my memory contains. Still, I know far more about the past than I know from memory. The most direct way to attain this further knowledge is through the memory of other men.

Here the problem of how we know the past touches upon the problem of understanding. Of the experiences of others, I know only so much as I can understand. A Chi-nese can relate his experiences to me, but only if we speak a common language. Hieroglyphics give information about the history of Egypt, but only to those who can read them. The experiences of a poet may be plainly re-vealed in his poetry, but only for those who themselves are capable of like experiences.

The memories of others to which I gain access through understanding draw on the treasures of the past far less completely than my own memory. My own memory con-tinues to come up with ever new details of which I did not think at first. Its limits cannot be drawn sharply. Of memory, too, it is truly said that at any given moment I am more than I know. But what I learn from others is limited. I know what I have learned and nothing more. At best, I may be able to make further conjectures, but they are not certain. The information that has come to me through understanding gives me knowledge and perhaps allows me a glance into another man's life. But it does not show me his life as a whole with all its hidden treasures.

This strangeness among men is the reason why often I do not understand even what I am told. The more of a stranger my informant is to me, the more will my understanding of what he tells me be limited to the mere facts. A mere fact, by definition, seems indeed to mean just the sort of thing that can be the common intellectual possession even of people who have no human understanding for each other. I know just how I felt during an experience I have had myself. But do I know how my grandfather felt as a child, or Charlemagne at his coronation, or Cheops while his pyramid was being built? All that is certain are the facts that my grandfather was a child once, that Charlemagne has been crowned, that the Cheops pyramid has been built.

My knowledge of the past becomes more and more indirect as I go on beyond my own memories, to the tale told by someone else, and on to the reading of a document. The indirectness grows still further when I rely on evidence that was not produced with the intent of giving information. I may find a piece of pottery from the Stone Age and draw the conclusion that there have been men who made this pottery. I may find the skull of a dinosaur and draw the conclusion that there lived an animal once that owned this skull. I may count the strata in sedimentary rock, and draw the conclusion that it took at least as many years to form the rock as there are layers. And just as we need human understanding, such as one man has for another, if we want to listen to a tale or read a document, we need our knowledge of causes and effects in nature if we want to draw the sort of conclusions I have mentioned. We need to know that pieces of pottery, skulls, and rock strata do not in nature come about of themselves, "by accident." The greater the precision with which we know what conditions must be met so that these objects may come into existence, the greater will be the precision with which we can draw from them conclusions about the past.

The transition from human understanding to causal conclusion is a gradual one. In the document I understand the meaning it carries, in the piece of pottery the intent of the potter, in the skull its objective usefulness to its former owner, in the layers of rock the course of nature according to her laws. The element that is diminishing with each step in this series I shall call subjective comprehensibility, that is, the comprehensibility that one subject has for another subject. We have reason to believe that subjective comprehensibility diminishes not merely because, in the remoter members of the series, man is no longer capable of comprehending a subjective content which is actually there. Rather, subjective comprehensibility decreases because a subjective content does in fact no longer exist. The piece of pottery was not made with the intent of communicating something. The skull was not formed by a conscious plan. And the layers of rock were never part of any living being, never served in anyone's struggle for survival.

Subjective comprehensibility is not at all the same thing as complexity. The earthen pot is far less complex than the skull. But the pot allows us a different approach—we can ask what was the intent of the potter. The skull, or even a honeycomb in a beehive, is created unconsciously by nature, in a way that is a mystery to us. The earthen pot, on the other hand, has come to be due to a conscious mind who to us is subjectively comprehensible. What is more, those objects that have come to be unconsciously are to begin with by far the more perfect things. Compare the highly complex hand of the Neanderthal man with the primitive stone wedge it has fashioned! Yet only consciousness becomes aware of the complexity of what has been created unconsciously. The hand itself has no knowledge of its own perfection, the sedimentary rock knows nothing of the laws of nature that have formed it. *Being is older than knowledge.* But on the other hand there is this truth which can no longer be expressed except as a tautology: *Only knowledge knows what being is.* These two statements about being and knowledge offer a sharper formulation of what I meant when I spoke of the circle of mutual dependence between subject and object.

At this point, many humanists insist on a sharp distinction. They say, true, we do understand man, but we do not understand inanimate nature. This is not the place to quibble over words. But it is important to me that we not forget the continuity and coherence that in reality exists among the cases which are conceptually separated by such a sharp borderline. Do we understand organic life? In the tenth chapter where we shall discuss animal psychology, I shall have occasion to show cause for my conviction that within certain limits we do indeed quite literally understand organic life. But I should not even consider it an unfortunate usage to say that we understand inanimate nature as well. When we understand a mathematical law of nature, we understand as much of nature as can be understood at all. And understandable in this sense is whatever is objectively related to the mind. Compare the unconscious performance of living things with that of inanimate nature! The grass grows, the bird flies, the bee builds its honeycomb, though they have never consciously learned how to do all this. They know how to do it without knowing what they are doing. But let us watch with a rested eye the flight of a stone we have thrown, or the course of a river, or the paths of the planets in the sky, and we shall see exactly the same miracle. The objects of inanimate nature, too, are able to do their part without knowing it. We know that their motions conform to differential equations that we are able to integrate only in a few simple instances. But these inanimate objects, without hesitation, without error, simply by their existence, are integrating the equations of which they know nothing. Subjectively, nature is not of the mind—she does not think in mathematical terms. But objectively, nature is of the mind—she can be thought in mathematical terms. This is perhaps the deepest truth we know of nature.

The last few sentences were meant to convey the frame of mind in which, I believe, we should approach the ultimate truth that will remain to us as we go back into the history of nature: the mathematical law of nature. But we must first deal with a methodical question that is involved in the application of the laws of nature to the remotest past. As I have said, remains such as an earthen sherd, a skull, or a rock stratum allow us to draw conclusions from them only if we know the conditions out of which, by the laws of nature, they have come into being. On the other hand, our knowledge of the laws of nature, and of the limits of their validity, is based exclusively on experience, and our experience of those distant times is derived entirely from these remains. Are we not caught up in circular reasoning when we test the laws of nature by the remains that we can interpret only with the help of these self-same laws?

This seeming circle, however, is of the very essence of the methods of the natural sciences generally. We always begin by assuming certain hypothetical laws, we then classify the phenomena of nature by these laws, and finally we confirm or disprove our initial hypothesis by observing whether the system we have built up in this manner produces contradictions. Tests of this sort have established with a very high degree of probability that the laws of nature as we know them today have been valid for the last two billion years. I shall give merely an indication how conclusions can be arrived at by this method. The kinship of some animals now long extinct and known only through fossil remains with species living today can be understood only on the assumption that the laws of organic chemistry were the same then as they are now. From the close relationship between old and young minerals, a like conclusion can be drawn for the laws of inorganic chemistry. But the chemical properties of a substance depend on very delicate traits in the structure of its atomic shells. This forces the conclusion that atomic physics was the same in detail then as it is now. Since all matter consists of atoms, it is difficult to conceive how the laws of nature could have undergone any appreciable changes at all. Even the gravitational constant that determines both gravitation on earth and the distance of the earth from the sun, cannot have changed too much in the last two billion years. Otherwise, conditions on the surface of the earth would have changed far more than is compatible with the continuous existence of normal rock stratification and of organic life. To be sure, conclusions of this sort are merely a piling up of probabilities. But that is all natural science can ever do.

How, then, can we determine the duration of past ages? Where do we get for the earth this minimum age of two billion years which I have mentioned several times?

Archeologists and geologists derive a relative chronology first of all from the position of stratified rock. Unless later disturbances have intervened, the higher strata are younger, the lower strata older. Whether two geological strata in different parts of the earth are of the same age, can be determined by the presence of the same index fossils in both strata. Index fossils are the remains of a species of animal or plant that has existed a short time only, but has been widely scattered over the face of the earth. Conclusions of this kind have allowed us to develop our present system of geological epochs. I lack the space here to explain all of the conclusions in detail.

How is this relative chronology finally turned into an absolute one? Where do we get the numbers for the years that we put on past events?

In human history we rely first of all on man's own calendars. Chroniclers from of old have been in the habit of recording the year in which an event has taken place. They may number the years beginning with the birth of Christ, or with the foundation of Rome, or with the ascension of the ruling king. In some cases we are able to connect their calendars with our own, exact to the day, by means of old reports of eclipses of the sun that our astronomers can identify.

We find our way many thousands of years back into the end of the last ice age by counting out the yearly strata in the so-called varved clays. These varved clays are the only sedimentary rocks in which the year when each layer was formed is beyond doubt, and which are found in sufficiently continuous deposits to allow us to establish a chronology.

The length of the various ice ages is estimated by an astronomical method that is still under dispute. Astronomical methods have been used to calculate the variations in the orbit of the earth, and the consequent variations in the intensity of solar radiation on earth. This method gives us indications of age that go back hundreds of thousands of years.

There is only one reliable method for the calculation of still more distant ages. That is the determination of the age of minerals containing radio-active elements, particularly uranium. Uranium, heaviest element in nature, changes slowly and spontaneously into lead. The change is due to the decay of the nuclei of the uranium atom. The atomic nuclei of both uranium and lead are composed of the same "elementary particles," that is, the same so-called neutrons and protons. The uranium nucleus, being the heavier one, contains the greater number of particles of both kinds. The electric repulsion that the protons in the nucleus exert on one another renders the uranium nucleus unstable. From time to time it spontaneously throws off some of its particles, and in this manner it finally changes through several intermediate stages into a lead nucleus. We cannot predict just when any one nucleus will accomplish the transformation. But there is a statistical law that governs the average length of life of uranium nuclei. This law says that of any given group of uranium nuclei half will decay every five billion years. It goes without saying that we have been able to observe the decay of uranium only over the short period of a few decades. But from the number of nuclei that have decayed in this short period, we can compute the number of nuclei that must decay over longer periods. Our conclusions are based on the fact that the decay is entirely independent of external influences such as temperature, pressure, or chemical reactions. And this fact, in turn, is in line with theory, for the decay goes on in the depths of the atomic nucleus and is accompanied by expenditures of energy of a scope which by comparison renders negligible all the external influences that we have mentioned and that affect the atomic shell only. Therefore, we may conclude that uranium has decayed evenly since the beginning of the earth.

Let us consider now a uranium mineral which has been formed long ago and which, to judge by its special kind of structure, did not take in any lead at the time of its formation. We find that this mineral today contains twenty percent lead. We understand this to mean that in the interval so and so many uranium atoms have changed into lead atoms. From the amount of lead now present we compute how long the process of decay has been going on, counting from the time when all of the atoms still were uranium atoms, and the result is: two billion years. This, then, is the age of the mineral.

It is obvious that this method of age determination must be used with extreme caution, and that it allows no more than very rough estimates. For throughout its long life, the fortunes of the mineral are subject to many changes. Supplementary methods of age determination have been developed, based on related principles. I shall not discuss the details. But I am asking the reader to think over with me the chronological tables that have grown out of all our methods of age determination.

Chronological tables are apt to seem playful. There is a certain charm in rambling through the sequence of events, a charm that makes us forget the seriousness of the single event indicated in our tables merely by a keyword and a number. Please do not forget this seriousness completely. I shall try to convey what a past of two billion years really means. We shall go back into the past in steps that, to begin with, cover the short length of ten years only, and that are lengthened tenfold at every tenth step. If I may use the expression: I am asking the reader to meditate through this sequence with me.

We all know what ten years may mean if we will just think back to what we have gone through these ten years past. The history of the world consists of decades not one of which could be left out. A ten year step from today takes us back into the years before the last war, another ten year step into the days of the League of Nations and the first ocean flights. Another step, and we are in the first world war, and so on through the years of peace that have long since grown strange to us, until a hundred years ago we find ourselves in the days of Palmerston and Metternich, the mid-Victorian times, the days of the first railroads. The technical advance that has made our world what it is today falls almost entirely within these hundred years.

We take hundred year steps. The sedate world of the nineteenth century now seems close to us. In the ten decades preceding it came into being much of the poetry that still lives for us today, and most of our music. A century earlier, and we are back in the Thirty Years' War. Past the Reformation and through the centuries of the Middle Ages we find our way back to King Arthur. These thousand years comprise the history of almost all the nations that now are the bearers of Western civilization.

We go back in thousand year steps. The same peoples that make up Europe today carried the Middle Ages. A thousand years earlier arose the ideas of order and of faith that have shaped the world since then. Roughly another thousand years earlier the first of those books were written that are moving us even today: Homer, the Old Testament, the Vedas, the Book of Transmutations. Three thousand years earlier, now six thousand years ago, the first great cultures came into being, and shortly before then the Ice Age ended in our latitudes.

Ten thousand years ago man was ignorant of metalcraft and of the art of writing. Twenty-five thousand years ago was the last high point of glaciation. A comparison with the preceding peak of glaciation seems to indicate that we are living now merely in one of the intervals between the great forward thrusts of the ice. Geologically speaking, we are living in the midst of the Ice Age. At some time during these hundred thousand years appears the species of man that we consider still closely related to us in physical characteristics. We call him *homo sapiens*. Was he mentally already similar to ourselves? If we were suddenly transported back into a state of nature, most of us would find that we do not possess the faculties of *homo sapiens* to which his stone instruments and his artistic creations bear witness. But how many tens of thousands of years have to go by before one small step forward is achieved! There can be no doubt that the tempo of the mind has become faster and faster. But the unconscious processes of life moved to the same measure then as they do now. Countless generations have succeeded one another in an unchanging sequence of birth, growth, and death.

A hundred thousand years ago, men of the Neanderthal type lived scattered over the earth. Where among them lived the ancestors of *homo sapiens* we do not know. The great ice ages followed one another in hundred thousand year cycles. Somewhere in these ice ages, or in the warmer intervals between them, we must place the discoveries of skulls and bones of the earliest beings whom we accept as men: the *sinanthropos* of Java, the Chinese *homo pekinensis*, the European *homo heidelbergensis*.

A million years ago the ice ages were just beginning. Going back two, three, ten million years we find ourselves still within the same geological epoch, youngest epoch of the youngest period, the Pliocene of the Tertiary. It seems as though only now we are emerging from the narrows of a history made up of catastrophes in rapid succession, into the spacious world of geological ages. These are the ages when the Alps, folded for some time in the depths of the earth, are slowly rising; when the temperature of the sub-tropical Tertiary is cooling down toward the Ice Age; when the animal species with whom we are still familiar, such as horse, cat, and ape, begin to take on the forms we know today.

Each of the epochs into which the Tertiary is subdivided extends over somewhat more than ten million years. The Oligocene, perhaps thirty-five million years ago, witnessed the peak of the subterranean folding activities that produced the great mountain chains of our earth, the Alps, the Andes, the Caucasus, and the Himalaya. Birds and the higher mammals begin to develop. Sixty to eighty million years ago, the Tertiary touches on the Cretaceous period in which the last dinosaurs walked the earth.

A hundred million years ago we are at the end of the so-called geological Middle Ages, two hundred million years ago at their beginning called Trias. Four hundred million years ago, life began to crawl from the sea onto dry land. About six hundred million years circumscribe the era in which we find traces of life and which, with the help of index fossils, can be divided into clearly distinct periods. Beyond the first of these periods, the Cambrian, lie those vast, little articulated expanses of time we call the pre-Cambrian period.

A billion years ago we are deeply in the pre-Cambrian period. Two billion years ago we are still in the pre-Cambrian period. The oldest known uranium minerals date from then. Recent research makes it seem likely that the earth is roughly three billion years old. If this is true, then the period in which we have found traces of life represents the most recent fifth of the history of the earth.

How did the world look before the earth came to be? The earth is a planet of the sun, one star among countless others. If we want to penetrate more deeply into the past, we must study the history of the stars. But before starting out on this venture we must know the setting. We must study the spatial structure of the universe.

III

The Spatial Structure of the Universe

W E SHALL find our way into the expanses of space
again by means of a tabulation. I shall arrange the
spatial dimensions known to contemporary science, in a
series of lengths each of which is ten times greater than
the preceding one. The short lengths are given only for
completeness, while the greater lengths require detailed
comments. My comments will be concerned in part with
the methods of astronomy for measuring distances, in part
with the objects that occupy those spaces.

10^{-13} cm, the ten-thousand-billionth part of a centi-
meter, is the shortest length known to present-day atomic
physics. We have reason to think that shorter lengths do
not exist, and that below this length the concepts of classical geometry cease being applicable to reality.

10^{-12} cm, ten times the shortest length known, is the
diameter of the larger atomic nuclei. Ten thousand times
as large, 10^{-8} cm, is the diameter of the atomic shells. Small
and large molecules, colloid particles, gas and dust particles
are combinations of atoms, and structures of this kind
form a series that reaches in size from the atomically small
to what we can see with the naked eye.

10^{-6} cm is approximately the size of the virus molecules which seem to represent an intermediate stage between animate and inanimate matter. Above 10^{-5} cm begin certain bacteria, the smallest living things in the specific sense of the word. From single-celled and many-celled beings we go on up until we arrive at the size of our own body. The sizes of the largest animals and plants are between 10 and 100 yards.

1 mile is the diameter of a small town, 10 miles or more that of a large town. 100 miles is a good drive. 1000 miles is the diameter of one of the large countries in Europe. The diameter of the earth is 7926 miles.

Here we stop. How and since when do we know the diameter of the earth?

The Greeks already knew that the earth has the shape of a ball—even though they never traveled round it. Eratosthenes of Alexandria determined the diameter of the earth by measurements that he was able to carry out without ever leaving Egypt. The Greeks were the first to realize that the science of geometry can be utilized to measure distances that we cannot pace off. All the distance measurements of astronomy are based on this realization.

How did Eratosthenes go about it? He knew that in Syene (today called Aswan), which lies on the Tropic of Cancer, the sun stands exactly in the zenith at noon of the longest day of the year. In that position, the sun shines to the bottom of a deep, vertical well without casting a shadow. He measured the length of the shadow cast by a vertical stick at the same hour, on the same day, in Alexandria which is 500 miles or 5000 stadia north of Syene. He found that in Alexandria the sun stood at this moment seven degrees (7°) south of the zenith. But objectively, the direction to the sun is the same in Syene as in Alexandria. For the distance to the sun is so great that the small shift of 500 miles becomes negligible by comparison. Consequently, the difference must be due to the fact that the zenith in Alexandria differs from that in Syene by seven degrees, because of the curvature of the earth. Now the direction of the zenith is merely a prolongation of the line from the center of the earth to the spot on the surface of the earth where one happens to be. Seen from the center of the earth, therefore, Alexandria and Syene are in two different directions, and these two directions form an angle of seven degrees. Let us suppose that a man traveled north from Syene, not just as far as Alexandria, but on along the meridian up to the north pole, then on the other side of the earth to the south pole, and from there north again along the same meridian back to Syene. An observer in the center of the earth, following the traveler with his eyes, would have to turn his head by a full three hundred and sixty degrees (360°). Hence, the straight distance of 5000 stadia between Syene and Alexandria must be the same fraction of the circumference of the earth, as the angle of 7° between the directions of the two cities is of the full circle of 360°. In this manner Eratosthenes was able to determine the circumference of the earth by measuring an angle and a distance. The error in his calculation amounted to twenty percent, an excellent accuracy if we consider that this was the first measurement of an entirely unexplored dimension.

Not quite two hundred and fifty thousand miles, or thirty times the diameter of the earth, is the distance to the moon. Ninety-three million miles, about four hundred times as far, is the sun. About three and one half billion miles away, forty times as far as the sun, is Pluto, farthest of the planets. A rifle bullet shot from the earth and traveling at uniform speed would reach the sun in about six years. The light from the moon arrives on earth in little over a second, that of the sun in eight minutes, the light of Pluto in six hours.

How did we measure these distances? Basically by the same method by which Eratosthenes found the circumference of the earth. The same object, seen from different points, appears in different directions. A tree by the roadside, seen from the various windows of a house, seems to stand in front of various points on the horizon. Seen from the windows of a moving railway coach, close objects go past quickly, distant ones slowly. The angle between the directions in which an object C is seen from point A and from point B is called the parallax of C with reference to the base AB. If I know the length of AB, I can figure out the distance of C from the base AB. Eratosthenes took the distance Alexandria-Syene as a base. The point whose position he wanted to determine was the center of the earth, and he proceeded indirectly by determining the direction of the two zeniths. The best method in measuring the distance of a planet is to choose two very distant points on the earth, because the longer the base, the more accurate the measurement. From this base, bearings can be taken upon the stars directly. I shall not go into details. The angles that have to be measured here are in the order of minutes, the error in the results is less than one percent.

The solar system is a small family of bodies that cosmically are closely related to each other. Going beyond this system ten times, or a hundred times, or a thousand times its diameter, we find nothing but empty space with a few meteorites and gaseous atoms scattered through it. Alpha Centauri, the nearest fixed star, is almost ten thousand times as far from the sun as Pluto. Distances of stars are measured in light-years. One light-year, or 5.87 million million miles, is the distance that light travels in one year. Alpha Centauri is four light-years away from us.

Even the distances of stars are still determined by the measurement of lengths and angles. The base we now use is the diameter of the orbit of the earth. For example, we might determine the direction of a star in the spring, and again in the fall. The distance between the positions of the earth in the two seasons is approximately 190 million miles. The directions in which the star is seen differ in all cases by less than one second, or less than the eighteen hundredth part of the angle that the diameter of the sun represents to our eye. The best parallaxes contain an error of probably less than ten percent.

If a star is over one hundred light-years distant, the angle becomes immeasurably small. But there are stars still much farther away. How can we measure their distance? Many methods have been developed, some based on the brightness of the star, some on its state of motion. I shall describe one of these methods as an example.

The basic idea of the method is that the distance of a star might be determined by a comparison of its "apparent" with its "true" brightness. "Apparent" we call the brightness with which we see the star in the sky, "true" the brightness that the star would show if it could be observed from a certain agreed standard distance. True brightness, then, is a unit of measurement for the energy of radiation that is objectively emitted by the star. Of two stars with the same true brightness, the star closer to us in space will appear brighter than the other. Apparent brightness is known by observation. If it were possible, now, to determine also the true brightness of the star, we should be able to compute the star's distance, by means of the law which governs the relation between distance and loss of brightness. But a star's true brightness is a symptom of the physical state of that star. Hence it is not surprising that the true brightness is closely linked to other physical characteristics of the star, some of which can be observed directly. A study of these characteristics allows us in many cases to determine the true brightness of a star, and therewith its distance. This method has been most successful in its application to the relation between the true brightness, and the period of fluctuation in the luminosity, of variable stars.

For not all fixed stars shine with unchanging brightness. A certain type of variable stars, named Cepheid variables after their best-known representatives Delta Cephei, shows absolutely regular fluctuations in brightness. The period of variation is characteristic for each star and does not change with time. Periods of various stars extend from fractions of a day upward to forty whole days. The cause of the variation is very probably the pulsation of the entire gaseous body of the star, a pulsation whose own cause we do not know so far. It has been found, now, that the true brightness of a star, and its period of variation, are uniquely related to each other. If one is known, the other can be computed. An adequate understanding of this relation is impossible, of course, until we know the causes of the pulsation. But even so, we may meanwhile use the relation in practice to determine distances. First, we must test the relation on stars whose distance is known by some other method. Then we can go on to more distant stars of which only the period of variation can still be observed, and determine their true brightness by means of the formula connecting the two factors. Since the Cepheid variables are among the stars of the greatest true brightness, we can with their help penetrate more deeply into space than by any other method.

When we have measured the distances, what have we learned?

The sun and all the stars visible to the naked eye belong to a large system whose most distant parts we see in the faint glimmer of the Milky Way all around us. We call it the Milky Way system or, with the Greek word, the Galaxy. It is shaped like a flattened lense, almost like a disk. Presumably it has spiral structure, but it is difficult to decide this point from our place of observation within the system itself. Its center is approximately fifteen thousand light-years away from us. Its size cannot be given with any accuracy, since it decreases in density in all directions and fades almost imperceptibly into empty space. The entire system could be put into a flat box ten thousand light-years high and one hundred thousand light-years in diameter. But the most distant, thin parts are often disregarded, and then smaller dimensions are given. According to rough estimates, the system contains one hundred billion luminous stars, every one of them comparable to our sun, and non-luminous matter adding up to about the same weight and mostly scattered through space in the form of gas or dust.

This system, again, is not alone in space. Small nebulous objects in the sky, many of which have spiral structure, turn out to be systems comparable to our Milky Way. We call them "nebulae" because of their appearance, but actually they consist mainly of stars. We shall come back to them in the sixth chapter. They are also called "extra-galactic" nebulae, to distinguish them from nebulae within the Milky Way. With our strongest telescopes we are still able to distinguish individual stars in the nebulae closest to us, in particular we can distinguish Cepheid variables that allow us to determine the distance of the nebulae. In this way we have found out that the best-known among them, the Great Spiral Nebula in Andromeda, is approximately seven hundred thousand light-years distant from us. In nebulae that are farther than this we can no longer distinguish individual stars. The method of measuring distance by apparent and true brightness is then applied to the nebula as a whole. Just as there are several types of stars, so there are several types of nebulae; shaped like a spiral, like an ellipse, like a Θ, irregular in shape, and so on. We know so far only a small part of the reasons for their various shapes. The sixth chapter contains some remarks on this point. But there is a certain relation between the type of a nebula and its true brightness, and so we are once more able to determine the distance of nebulae from their type and their apparent brightness. To be sure, the results of this method are by now already quite inaccurate. For the larger distances we may have to count with an error of fifty percent.

With our telescopes we can see somewhere around one hundred million nebulae. By and large, they are evenly distributed through space, but in some places they combine in loose clusters. The farthest visible nebulae are around five hundred million light-years away, that is, about a thousand times as far as the Great Nebula in Andromeda. There is nothing to prevent us from assuming that further improvements of our telescopes will allow us to see still more distant nebulae. Their fairly even distribution up to the limits of observable space seems to indicate that what we have observed is only a small segment of much larger spaces, full of nebulae.

The manner in which the nebulae move forces us to conclude that they, in turn, are only parts of a larger, physically coherent system. We can tell whether a body moves away from us or toward us, from a shift in the vibration of the light that the body emits. We all are familiar with this phenomenon from our experiences with sounds. An airplane flying toward us gives off a high sound which suddenly becomes deeper as the plane has passed overhead and is now flying away from us. We can make the same observation with a whistling locomotive. The more sound waves reach our ear per second, the higher the sound. If the plane is coming closer, there is, indeed, a greater number of sound waves reaching our ear than would be the case if the plane, for instance, were standing still. For the sound waves sent out later have a shorter path to travel than those sent out earlier, therefore, the time intervals with which they reach our ear are shorter than the intervals with which they left the plane. The fact that the plane is coming closer compresses the sound waves for the observer who is standing still, while when the plane is moving away the sound waves are extended, drawn apart. In the same way, the number of light waves arriving per second increases when the source of light is coming closer, and decreases when the source of light is moving away. Now an increase in the rate of light vibrations means that the spectral lines of the light are displaced toward blue, a decrease that they are displaced toward red.

Practically all extra-galactic nebulae show a displacement of the spectral lines toward red, and the farther the nebula is away, the greater the displacement it shows. We must be cautious, of course, in applying to those most distant objects notions that have served well when applied to objects near by. But for reasons I cannot here discuss in detail I am inclined to think that in this instance we can proceed without hesitation. The rest of this chapter is based on that assumption. We must conclude, then, that all nebulae are moving away from us, and that they are moving away with a speed which increases the farther away they are. The highest speed we have been able to discover in this manner is over one tenth the speed of light. The universe we know is expanding.

It would be strange if our position in the universe enjoyed special treatment. Why, then, do all the nebulae move away just from us, while we ourselves seem to be standing still? This, however, is merely an illusion. In reality, every nebula is moving away from every other nebula, and that is the only reason why all of them are also moving away from us. An observer on any other nebula would gain exactly the same impression, namely that the whole universe is concentrically moving away from him. When we stretch a rubber band, every point on it, too, is moving away from every other point, and only an outside observer can tell which of them is in reality standing still. Which of the nebulae might possibly be considered the center of the whole system—that is a question we shall be able to answer only when we can observe the limits of the system, that is, the most distant nebulae. We cannot do so now, hence it remains uncertain whether the system has any limits and, consequently, whether it has any center at all.

Probably the most adequate and clearest illustration of the movement of the nebulae is furnished by the comparison with the scattering blast fragments of an explosion. At a certain moment after the explosion, those fragments that travel fastest must obviously have covered the greatest distance. The result would be exactly the same relation between distance and speed that we have observed in the nebulae. The physical significance of this illustration I shall discuss in the next chapter.

The last distance contained in our tabulation of the spatial structure of the universe is a hypothetical radius of the world, three billion light-years. I do not attach much importance to this purely speculative figure. But since it has been mentioned I shall explain it. This radius can be arrived at by two methods. According to a law of the special theory of relativity, no mass can move faster than light. Now the speed of the nebulae is growing in proportion to their distance from us. If we apply this proportion of speed to distance, to objects still more distant from us (and so far not observed), nebulae at a distance of three billion light-years must be traveling with the speed of light. Since faster nebulae are not supposed to exist, this distance would then mark the end of the nebulae or, at any rate, the end of the space in which the relation between speed and distance is valid.

The estimate just explained is in surprising agreement with another estimate derived from the general theory of relativity. In the general theory, the universe may be conceived as a closed structure of finite volume whose two-dimensional analogue would perhaps be the surface of a globe. The "curvature" of this space is given in the medium density of matter. I do not want to go more deeply into these problems, since they are beyond what is empirically well established, while in this chapter I want to stay as much as possible within this framework. I may add merely that the best estimates of the radius of the world, based on the general theory of relativity, arrive at approximately the same figure that we found earlier from observation of the spiral nebulae. This seems to indicate that both approaches share a common core of truth.

IV

The Time Structure of the Universe

CHRONOLOGICAL tables of the history of the universe I cannot give. We do not know enough for that. But we do possess one important piece of knowledge, namely, that such tables would probably reach no further into the past than the tables of the history of the earth itself. If we define the universe cautiously as a world similar in nature to the world we know today, made up of stars and star systems of the kind familiar to us, we may then state with a high degree of probability: the universe is no older than about five billion years.

In this chapter, I shall first present the arguments supporting this particular estimate of the age of the universe. Later I shall discuss the general law from which it follows that the events in this world are unique, irreversible, and of finite duration, in short, that the world is historic: the Second Law of thermodynamics. The pages devoted to the Second Law will make greater demands on the reader's capacity and inclination for abstract thought than most of the rest of the book.

The estimates of the age of the world fall into three large groups. They are based, either on the movement of the extra-galactic nebulae, or on the evolution of certain types of stars and star systems, or, finally, on the decay of radio-active atomic nuclei.

Let me take up with the closing remarks of the preceding chapter. I said that the nebulae are flying away from one another like the blast fragments of a gigantic explosion. We know the speed with which the nebulae are moving. We know the distance they must have covered since they separated, namely, their present distance from one another. From this information we can compute the moment when the explosion must have taken place. The result of our computation is a moment in time two billion years ago.

Both the question whether this computation is fundamentally justified, and the accuracy of the result are open to doubt. The fundamental doubt would concern our interpretation of the displacement of the spectral lines as an indication of motion. The doubt of the accuracy would concern, not so much the basic observations which are rather well established, as the question whether the nebulae have in the past traveled with the same speed as today. I shall defer both problems until we have discussed other methods of age determination.

Until quite recently, the evolution of stars and star systems was a field for conjecture and speculation. Accordingly, the age estimates given for stars and star systems were of motley variety. As our figures become more certain, they show more and more clearly that there is at least an upper age limit for all the objects in the universe, and that there is nothing to compel us to set this limit higher than a few billion years. There are objects, of course, which in their present form are definitely younger, but there are none which are definitely older. I can devote only a few short sentences to the great wealth of studies in this field. The sixth and seventh chapters will contain a little more about the empirical and theoretical background of age estimates.

It is certain that the earth is at least as old as the oldest minerals found on it today, that is, at least two billion years. I have said earlier that the most recent estimates based on radio-active methods set the age of the earth at three billion (3×10^9) years. Since we have discovered the sources of the sun's atomic energy, we know that the sun's present rate of radiation certainly cannot have been maintained in the past for more than about thirty billion years, though it may be any number of years less. The same considerations give us upper limits for the possible ages of most stars, ages which are similarly far beyond the presumable age of the world. But certain very bright stars consume their energy so quickly that their present radiation cannot have lasted longer than ten million (10^7) years. Thus, in their present form, they must be a hundred times younger than the earth. The study of the stability of rotating masses reveals that the spiral nebulae probably cannot be older than a few billion years, and that very rapidly rotating but otherwise normal stars cannot be older than some ten million years. Earlier estimates, based on the evolution of double stars and similar systems, and apparently demanding much higher ages, have become doubtful in the light of more recent theories.

Radio-active matter furnishes much more precise figures. In the second chapter I explained how radio-active matter helps us to determine the age of minerals. The same method has been used to determine the age of meteorites that have fallen on the earth. The highest age found for them is around six billion years. But we can also estimate the age of radio-active atoms themselves. There are very weighty reasons for the assumption that such atoms do not originate in the portion of the universe that we know, nor have originated in it as long as it has been in its present state. But these radio-active atoms decay as time goes on. It follows that the physical matter we know must at one time have been in a state in which radio-active atoms could originate. The appearance of radio-active atoms probably required either temperatures of around one hundred million degrees centigrade—temperatures that we cannot expect to encounter even among the stars in existence today—or some other equally drastic variation from the present state of the world. If we estimate the age of radio-active atoms by their present frequency of occurence and their rate of decay, we arrive at figures in the neighborhood of four billion years.

What conclusions shall we draw from these figures? First, let us consider the fact that they are all of the same order of magnitude, and then let us study their differences in detail.

The fact that estimates for such a variety of objects in the universe, based on such different methods, give ages of a few billion years, seems to indicate that the world in its present state is actually not older than that. The figures support each other by their agreement. Their agreement is for me the decisive reason why the displacement toward red in the spectra of the nebulae should be interpreted as an indication of the movement of the nebulae.

The differences among the various figures may in part be due to still existing inaccuracies in their determination. In part, the differences may indicate that the various objects really do differ in age. At all events, the earth must be younger than the atoms composing it. And insofar as our figures can be accorded this degree of accuracy, it seems permissible to draw from them a more accurate picture of the sequence of events in the origin of the world. In this respect, however, we are still in the beginnings. If we allow our figures so much weight, they show contradictions in detail that are still unexplained. Above all, it appears that the age of the entire known world is somewhat shorter than the well-established age of certain objects within the world, such as the earth, or meteorites. As long as these difficulties have not been resolved, I shall abstain from offering hypotheses about the details of the origin of the world once long ago. What details are necessary as a background for the history of the star system are given in the sixth chapter.

We must now raise the question what may have been the historic rank order of those events that occurred billions of years ago. I have called them the origin of the universe, the beginning of the world. Have I a right to do this? One of the most important steps in the development of natural science was taken when science left behind the myths of the creation of the world and conceived the idea of a world of eternal duration. Do the data I have just reviewed offer a reason for taking this step back? All forms existing in the universe may be of finite age—but why should they not have grown out of other forms? The events of billions of years ago, why should they have been anything more than a transformation? I want to stress specifically that not one of the considerations I have offered compels us to assume that new matter had come into existence. Even the formation of radio-active atoms can easily be understood as a building-up process out of lighter atoms already in existence, hydrogen atoms for example. Does our universe perhaps pass through a periodic round of world conflagrations after which everything starts over again from the beginning?

Obviously, we have no final answers to such questions. We lack one essential prerequisite, the knowledge, namely, whether the laws of nature as we know them were equally valid in those most distant ages. However, once we assume the permanent validity of a few of our most basic laws of nature, mainly of the Second Law of thermodynamics, we are able to give an unequivocal answer to our question. With the Second Law, and one simple and plausible assumption besides, it can be proved that the world is a sequence of events incapable of repetition, in which for every finite quantity of matter there is also only a finite quantity of distinguishable, unique events. The exact meaning of this statement will be explained later on. First, I want to mention the aspects under which the statement is important to me.

Whether or not at some time in the future my statement is to encounter limits to its validity, it does state the internal law of the world's course as far as we know it: the historic character of nature. It also shows how fundamental are the assumptions that we would have to give up if we were to assume an infinite sequence of events. On the other hand, it has the weakness of every general statement, namely that it does not give a concrete model of the process which it asserts in general terms. That is why I have started out with concrete considerations about the age of the world. The flight of the nebulae as from an explosion, the formation of stars, and the decay of radio-active atoms are examples of a historic, irreversible process in the sense of my statement. But there remains something arbitrary in postulating this relation between the general law and the model. The general law may be illustrated by the model, but the specific features of the model cannot be derived from the general law alone. In particular, even though the general law claims that the world has had a beginning, it remains uncertain whether the beginning to which the model can be traced is really the true beginning of the world. The true beginning may lie further back. Furthermore, the beginning may not have been a sharply marked event. I shall come back to these problems at the close of the chapter.

In order to understand the Second Law of thermodynamics, we must start with the first law, the law of the conservation of energy. The first law states that the energy content of a closed system does not change with time. Energy is here defined as the capacity to perform mechanical work such as lifting a weight. Mechanical work can be measured, for example by multiplying the weight of the matter that is raised with the distance by which it is raised. The energy content of a body is the amount of work the body is able to perform. Since it is difficult to know when the energy content of a body is completely exhausted, it is safer to deal only with changes in energy content. A change in the condition of a body, for instance a chemical reaction, means a certain change in its energy content. This change is measured by measuring the amount of work required to bring about the change, or, if the change is spontaneous, by measuring the amount of work the body can perform while undergoing the spontaneous change. A closed system is defined as a physical structure that does not exchange any energy with its surroundings. According to the first law, such a system cannot either gain or loose energy. If a structure gives off energy, or if it receives energy from outside, then, according to the first law, its energy content must change in proportion. Consequently, energy—at first defined merely as a capacity, the capacity to perform work—can now be treated in our calculations as if it were a substance. In this lies the value of the law of the conservation of energy for physical science.

We know many forms of energy. The simplest example is kinetic energy, that is, the energy of motion. A fast moving car can perform work—it rolls a little stretch up-hill after its motor has been cut off, and so lifts its own weight. Among other forms of energy we know, for instance, the energy of gravity, contained in the raised weight itself; the chemical energy of fuels or explosives; electric energy; the energy of atomic nuclei; and finally the form of energy that is the most important one for us here: heat. The various forms of energy can be converted each into the others. In a steam engine, chemical energy is converted into heat and heat into kinetic energy. What remains constant in a closed system is not the amount of energy in any one of its forms, but rather the total amount of energy in whatever form.

The Second Law is concerned with the conversion of heat into other forms of energy. Let us limit our considerations to the conversion of heat into kinetic energy and vice versa. The steam engine shows that heat can turn into kinetic energy, and the heating of a body by friction shows that kinetic energy can turn into heat. But the relation between kinetic energy and heat is not altogether symmetrical. A body can turn its entire kinetic energy into heat, for instance, when it is brought to a complete stop by friction. But a body cannot turn its entire heat content into kinetic energy. The steam in the engine, at best, cools down to the temperature of its surroundings. The heat energy that is then left in the steam can no longer be turned into work, since the excess pressure in the cylinder was due only to the excess temperature of the steam. Only differences in temperature are capable of performing work; heat that is evenly distributed is a form of energy which may well be the result of work, but which cannot be converted back into work. Hence, the production of heat is to some extent irreversible. We have defined a certain term, called entropy, as a measure of that heat content of a body which is no longer capable of performing work. With the help of this term, the Second Law may now be formulated as follows: The entropy of a closed system may increase or remain constant, but it cannot decrease. As long as no other forms of energy are converted into heat it remains constant. Otherwise, it increases.

Since practically every event in nature produces heat—

though often very small amounts—every event is in the strictest sense irreversible. Every pendulum comes to a stand-still. Even the motion of the planets around the sun is constantly slowed down ever so little by inter-stellar gas. Hence, no event in nature is repeated ex-actly. Nature is a unique course of events. The final state would be one in which all motion has come to rest, in which all differences in temperature have been equalized. This state has been called "heat death." Every closed system on earth, excepting only long-lived radio-active matter, reaches this state within observable time. That the course of events on earth continues at all is possible only because there is a constant influx of energy in the rays of the sun—in other words, only because the earth is not a closed system. But given enough time, no structure in the universe should be able to escape heat death. It is con-ceivable, of course, that certain forms of energy, such as the energy of atomic nuclei or the kinetic energy of stellar bodies moving in empty space, would never be converted into heat at all. But even then, there would be in the end no longer any conversion of energy.

Against the application of the Second Law to the world as a whole, the objection has been raised that the world as a whole may not be a closed system—for instance, if it is unlimited in extent. But this theoretical objection does not change much our concrete conclusions. The course of events in a finite part of the world could continue for-ever only if energy were forever flowing into it from the surroundings. As far as we know the world, there is no such influx of energy. On the contrary, all the stars are constantly losing energy by radiation into empty space.

The concrete model of the universe of which I spoke above is surely moving toward heat death. When I said earlier that the uniqueness of the course of the world could be established with the help of one simple supplementary assumption, I meant this assumption that no unlimited supplies of heat are being furnished to the world from outside.

It might be said, however, that the Second Law is merely a special empirical law of terrestrial physics, and that nothing compels us to accord it equal validity for far-off spaces and times in the universe. I should answer, first, that we are already applying the Second Law in astrophysics, with good success. Of course, this fact alone does not prove that the Second Law remains valid even beyond the limits of our knowledge in space and time. But I might say further that the Second Law is not just any empirical law. In fact, it can be derived from principles so basic that it would be difficult to conceive the possibility of circumstances so different that the law would be no longer valid. This derivation of the Second Law is supplied by what is called its statistical interpretation.

Heat—or to be more exact, that physical state which produces the sensation of heat—is a disordered movement of the atoms. This fact is now well established experimentally. Hence, heat energy is really kinetic energy. When a moving body because of friction converts its kinetic energy into heat, the atoms in the body do not thereby stop moving. Before, they were all moving in the same direction, thus producing the visible movement of the whole body. Now, each atom is moving to and fro restlessly within a small space, while only the center of gravity of the body is at rest. What appears to us as a transition from motion to heat is actually a transition from ordered to disordered motion. Expressed in these terms, the Second Law states that ordered motion can be converted completely into disordered motion, but that disordered motion cannot be converted completely into ordered motion.

In order to make this statement exact and thereby capable of prof, we must find a mathematical definition for the concept of disorder. We must find a way to measure the degree of disorder. This is accomplished by the distinction between macro-states and micro-states. The macro-state of a body we call the state of the body such as it is defined by its directly measurable thermodynamic characteristics like pressure, temperature, density, etc. A body whose thermodynamic characteristics are known is in a well-defined macro-state. But the micro-state of the same body could be defined only with the help of measurements of ultra-microscopic precision and completeness. We shall assume that the micro-state of the body is characterized by the indication of both the position and the speed of every single atom in the body. In practice, micro-states can never be known, they can only be delimited statistically. To this end they are correlated to certain macro-states. There is, of course, a certain macro-state corresponding to every micro-state, since the behavior of all the atoms together determines the values of the gross characteristics that can be measured. But it is not true that there is one single micro-state corresponding to every macro-state. There are many more different micro-states than macro-states. For example, the temperature of a body indicates the average kinetic energy of the caloric motion of its atoms—but in a total of 10^{23} atoms, there is a large number of different states of motion each of which has the same average kinetic energy per atom.

The number of different micro-states corresponding to one certain macro-state can be used, now, as a characteristic in the definition of that macro-state. The micro-states cannot be distinguished from one another "macroscopically," but actually they are different. Their number is called the thermodynamic probability of the macro-state. This term expresses the thought that, the greater the number of micro-states in a given macro-state that we shall call A, the greater is the probability that any micro-state chosen at random will belong to this macro-state A. This thermodynamic probability, now, is the measuring rod of disorder for which we have been looking. Ordered motion is one whose macroscopic characteristics already indicate its micro-state with great accuracy. For example, if the only motion of the atoms in a body is represented by the motion of the body as a whole, then I know the direction and speed of all the atoms as soon as I know the direction and speed of the body as a whole. In this case, there is one single micro-state corresponding to the macro-state, and the motion is completely ordered motion. On the other hand, in a macro-state of very high thermodynamic probability, the knowledge of the characteristics of the macro-state tells us almost nothing about the motion of the atoms. In that case, the state of motion is greatly disordered.

The Second Law, now, follows from considerations of

probability. Let us assume we are dealing with a body which, at a certain moment, is in a macro-state A of relatively low thermodynamic probability. For brevity let us say that the body is in an improbable state. In what direction is this state likely to change? We can neither watch nor predict in detail the motions of the individual atoms. Thus, we can say only that the body is going to change into some other micro-state of which we know beforehand merely that it will be one of the possible states close to state A—a state, that is, whose macroscopic characteristics are not too much different from those of A. Among these neighboring states there must be those with a higher and those with a lower thermodynamic probability. The most probable thing is obviously that the body will change into one of those states whose probability is higher than that of A. Consequently, in the majority of cases the change will go in the direction of higher probability. The body will keep on changing in that direction, on and on, until it reaches finally the state of highest probability. In that state it is then going to remain. Now the body has the maximum of disordered motion, that is, of heat: it has achieved "heat death."

These reflections show that the course of events claimed by the Second Law occurs not with certainty but merely with probability. But the number of atoms is so tremendously large that variations from the statistical mean occur practically never, except in microscopically small bodies. Speaking merely in terms of energy, it is possible that a stone on the ground cooled off suddenly and, with the help of the kinetic energy freed by the cooling, jumped up into the air. But this has never happened, and never will. There has not been enough time since the beginning of the world for such an event even to become probable to any appreciable degree. It is still less probable that large portions of the world should reverse their direction of development. Entropy, it has turned out, is a measure of thermodynamic probability (namely, its logarithm). Consequently, the law that originally ran thus: It is probable that the thermodynamic probability of a body's state will increase—this law may now be formulated empirically: It is certain that the entropy of a body will increase.

Physicists have a habit of using commonplace or quaint examples to illustrate an abstract train of thought. Let us suppose a vast desert in which Arabs on their camels are riding hither and thither. In this desert there is a small hill. We define a "micro-state" for each Arab by indicating precisely the spot where he just happens to be. But we shall call "macro-state" the indication whether the Arab is on the hill or not. The macro-state "not on the hill" is far more probable than the macro-state "on the hill," since the size of the hill is very small compared with that of the entire desert. If the Arab is on the hill today, I can predict practically with certainty that he will not be on the hill tomorrow. Entropy acquires the highest possible value, if it does not have it already, and retains that value if it has it. That all the Arabs should meet on top of the hill by chance is virtually impossible. But if they should have met there once—for instance, by appointment—they will soon afterward be scattered all over the desert. Such is the probability of increase in disorder. What is more, we must remember that the Arabs, as conscious beings, can decide to do something improbable, while the atoms cannot.

It is difficult to conceive of circumstances that would invalidate the statistical proof of the Second Law. Fundamentally, there are fewer empirical elements in this law than in any other law of physics. However, I want to call attention to a premise of the Law that is often overlooked. That is the structure of time which, in the opening chapter, I have called the historic character of time.

Let us study once more the improbable macro-state A. We assume this state to prevail at this moment. To the question, in what state will this body be in the immediate future, the answer must be: In a more probable macro-state. That is the Second Law. But if we ask, in what state has this body been in the immediate past, the answer, apparently with the same degree of probability, is once more: In a more probable macro-state. For if the Arab is on the hill today, it is equally probable that he has not been there yesterday, and that he will not be there tomorrow. Yet it is obvious that our example fails when applied to the past. The answer we get for the past is empirically false. It contradicts the Second Law. According to the Second Law, the probability of a state is constantly increasing. Therefore, in the immediate past the body must have been in a less probable state than it is now. Why is it that the same method of drawing conclusions is true for the future, and false for the past?

The conclusion rests on the idea of probability. Probability is the quantitative expression of the idea of possibility. Future events are possible. This is why it makes sense to ask how probable they are. Past events are factual.

We simply do not ask with what degree of probability this or that past event would lead up to the present, because the event has already occurred. There is no need to "predict" the event with a certain degree of probability, for it is known, or at least can be known, with certainty.

At first, these considerations show merely that we cannot draw conclusions of this sort with reference to the past, since of the past more is known than of the future. Probability, clearly, is an idea that is meaningful only where there is no certainty. But that the Second Law must necessarily have been just as valid in the past can be proved by the reflection that every moment in the past was at one time a moment in the present, and at that time conclusions about the future had to be based on probability. The historic character of time is usually assumed with a naïveté that causes us to overlook its importance in establishing the Second Law.

These reflections will make it clear that the historic character of time is far from being merely a subjective quality of human experience. Or conversely, we might say these reflections show how impossible it is for us even to conceive of the objects of physics without referring them to a subject capable of knowing them. Atomic physics has made this fact familiar to us. In reality, however, our reflections show how unnatural is a system which on principle separates subject and object—as classical natural science did. As far as the Second Law is concerned, however, we may conclude that if we were to abandon it for the distant past, or for the distant future, we would by implication be assuming that in those distant ages the past does not consist of what has happened and is factual, and the future does not consist of what is to come and is possible.

Can we at last arrive at a more concrete conclusion about the beginning of the world? Every finite part of the world has only a finite number of clearly distinguishable macro-states. Since every part passes through each of its states only once, it also has only a finite reserve of possible distinguishable "events." In this formulation, the revolution of one star around another in a manner that does not change for millions of years is not considered as an event but as a stable macro-state. If events follow upon each other with finite speed, they must also run out in finite time. It follows, not only that there is an end in heat death awaiting the events, but also that events must have had a beginning in time. It is equally easy to conceive that events have begun all at once, or that they have grown slowly out of infinite eventless time, asymptotically, in the same manner in which heat death is generally reached. How meaningful it would still be to apply the concept of time to an eventless interval, that is a question which I shall leave open.

V

Infinity

IN THE preceding chapter we have gone together up to the limit of our knowledge of space and time. What lies beyond that limit?

The question throws us into a strange dilemma. We do not know what lies beyond that limit, or else it would not be the limit of our knowledge. Still, we assume that something does lie beyond it. And this alone is already an assumption about something we do not know. Our assumption becomes even more specific as we are trying to imagine what there is beyond the limit of our knowledge. With what right dare we pass the limit in this fashion?

We do it with exactly the same right with which we conjecture into the future. The dialectics of the limits of our knowledge, and the dialectics of the idea of possibility, are closely related. The question whether something that is not, can be or cannot be, seems just as doubtful, but it does make sense at least if we ask whether something that is not, will be in the future. In a like manner we may hope to know at some future time what we do not know today. Similar, also, are the methods by which we can find answers to our two questions for what is not yet, and for what we do not yet know. We dare predict the future, once we have discovered a principle in what has happened until now. Similarly, we grope our way forward into the unknown, by means of the laws we have discovered in the area of what is known.

The assumption we have made in the two preceding chapters may serve as an example. Concerning the distribution in space of the nebulae we assumed that the segment of space we know is only a relatively small part of a larger space filled with nebulae. The fact that their distribution in space is of uniform density up to the limits of our knowledge, allows us to assume that we have discovered something like a law—a law that is not going to stop being valid just at the entirely accidental point where the power of our telescopes gives out. Conversely, we assumed that the universe as we know it did not exist before certain events that happened several billion years ago. For the flight of the nebulae away from one another, and the decay of radio-active atoms, proceed by laws that do not allow for the unchanged extension of these processes back into the past.

Reflections like these can establish, beyond the limits of our knowledge, an advance territory of well-founded assumptions. But these assumptions, too, fade finally into the unknown. And so there is a limit, however ill-defined, beyond which even our assumptions do no longer carry. What lies beyond that limit?

Must we refuse this question? May we not at least suppose with good reason that there is still something there beyond the limit of our well-founded assumptions, even though we have no notion what? Could it be that our thoughts, by the mere assumption that there is still something there, are capable of making well-founded assumptions that go beyond all limits? The concepts of infinite space and of infinite time give concrete form to this idea. We shall hardly ever be able to know what there is beyond all limits in space and time. But, at least, must not space and time themselves go on into infinity?

The two preceding chapters will have made it clear that science today is quite skeptical of these suppositions. It has accepted the possibility that beyond certain limits our very concepts of space and time cease being applicable. For it was science first of all that taught us to apply the concepts of space and time to areas which probably have never been accessible to the immediate perception of any conscious being that led its existence within the forms of experience of space and time. So far as there still exist bodies that can serve as measuring rods, and so long as there are still events that can serve to measure time, we are free to speak of spaces and of times whose extent, or course, no conscious being has ever perceived. But when we come into spheres whose laws no longer admit measuring rods and time clocks, then space and time turn into abstract and presumably meaningless constructions. Particularly, if we now find new laws that can be expressed only after we have surrendered certain features of our ideas of space and time, then, it seems to us, there is nothing to keep us from making that surrender.

If one discusses such thoughts here and there with others, he may have a startling experience. Few questions are as remote from our everyday needs as are these—yet few can arouse more heated debates. Almost invariably, these debates end inconclusively as regards the issue itself. But they are not without result, though on a different level, the level of human existence. The position taken to these problems reveals human attitudes, human types, and if we know a man well we can often tell beforehand what position he will take. The believer, the doubter, the dreamer, the zealot, the pedant—each will react in his own way. Man tries to penetrate into the factual truth of nature, but in her last, unfathomable reaches suddenly, like in a mirror, he meets himself.

Please do not shun the look into this mirror. It tells us something not just about ourselves as individuals, but also about the unconscious assumptions of our age. And it also takes us part of the way around that side of the subject-object circle which I cannot trace elsewhere in this book. We shall still have to talk so much, in the self-assured terms of natural science, about nature itself, and about man's dependence on nature, that we may well allow ourselves here to be reminded that our ideas of nature depend upon our own personality and upon the spirit of our age. I shall proceed historically and, as far as can be done in one short chapter, relate and interpret the answers that the Western world since ancient Greece has given to the problem of infinity.

Let us begin with myth. Long before the awakening of what we call the rational explanation of nature, man described his immediate surroundings in terms much like those we are using. The objective conditions of a peasant's life were little different in the days of Helen of Troy from what they are today. But the outer limits of man's existence are usually marked with mighty imagery, differing with the nature of the people and with its state of development. I shall choose Greek mythology as an example for them all.

Hesiod relates: In the beginning lived the men of the Golden Age, carefree and happy. The men of the Silver Age followed, eternal children. Then came the men of the Bronze Age, those mighty heroes, and finally come we of the Iron Age, living under the yoke of sweat and toil. As we look back into the past, the paradisiac state in the beginning arrests our eye. The essence of that state is timelessness, symbolized by the bliss and length of life of man in those days. Is it at all possible to inquire beyond it?

If we inquire beyond man, we come into the region of the gods. In the beginning were the original deities, Uranos and Gaia, heaven and earth. From their eternal embrace have sprung all creatures. After them Cronos ruled, followed by the Olympic Zeus, lord of our world. Heaven and earth—that is the whole universe. The gods placed at the beginning of the universe tower as images beyond whom no question may be asked. The mythical formula: "In the beginning was . . ." sets at the beginning something changeless, something to which our ideas of time cannot be applied.

The idea of space is similar. The earth is a round disk around which flows the river of Oceanos. This image, also, has mythical significance. Oceanos is at the same time a god, but he belongs to the Titans, that older race of gods which is opposed to the Olympians, the gods of measure and mean. Man, subject of the Olympians, cannot enter the region of Oceanos. And so the question what lies beyond Oceanos, or what was before heaven and earth, this question does not just remain unanswered—it is sacrilege.

Greek philosophy raised the question of the world's extent in space and of its duration. According to Aristotle the world is finite in extent. In its center is the ball-shaped earth, its outer boundary is the sphere of the fixed stars. Outside that sphere there is no thing and hence no place, since every place is the place of some thing. The idea of space as such, existing even if it is not filled by some thing, was unknown to the Greeks—with the exception of the atomistic school. Within the framework of this image, Greek astronomy has given a description of what stars had been observed, and passed it on to later ages under the name of Ptolemy.

There were diverse opinions about the age of the world. According to Aristotle, the world is un-created and imperishable. This shows that the Greeks did not think in finite terms only, neither on principle nor by preference. Yet there is a common principle to be found in Aristotle's divergent notions of the spatial and temporal extent of the world, and that is the principle that whatever is, is comprehensible. To Aristotle it seemed impossible to think of a world extending into infinity without getting involved in contradictions, but just as impossible to think of a beginning or end of the world in time. And that which is unthinkable cannot be. This world-view is strictly rational. All symbolic ideas have disappeared from it. But in its rational lucidity it is itself a symbol of the Greek belief that whatever is, is comprehensible.

The Christian Middle Ages adopted Ptolemy's image

of a world finite in space. They added to it the doctrine of the world's finite duration. The world is contained in the time span between Creation and Judgment Day, just as the Bible is contained between Genesis and Apocalypse. The image of the world is once again defined in mythical terms. But no myth is accidental. The new image of the temporal process reflects a new content. In contrast to antiquity, Christianity thinks essentially in historic terms. The fate of mankind must be understood under the all-embracing aspect of the history of salvation. But if history was conceived as a meaningful whole, it could not be conceived other than finite. Creation, man's fall, redemption, and judgment are the sole important themes of the history of the world, and they unfold in finite time.

The world's finitude is an expression of the essence of the world in still another way. God is infinite, the world is finite—this is the true relation between God and the world. Classical antiquity experienced the order of the world in its encompassable finiteness. Even the Olympic gods are finite. But in late antiquity, man suffered more and more under the burden of the world's finiteness. The god who delivers from this agony is the infinite God of Christianity. But he does not deliver man by transposing him beyond reality. Man's longing for infinity, for boundlessness, is first met with a boundless demand: Thou shalt be perfect like thy Father in Heaven. In the face of this demand, the suffering from our natural limitations pales beside the experience of our self-limitation through our own failure, our own fault. And the deliverance is love that breaks through the boundaries between man and man, and between man and God. Divine grace comes to man when love acts within him. And the essence of God's infinity is that God is love.

Modern times have conceived the world as infinite in both time and space. This infinity has a twofold significance. It opens up a field for inquiry and conquest, and at the same time it is a symbol. Clearly the limits of the medieval world-view had to be torn down to give us access to the facts of outer reality. The modern age begins with Columbus and Copernicus, for they went beyond limits. The Christian myth had to give way to the new science. On the heels of science, technology followed. Modern man thinks he can breathe freely only if his conquest of the world is no longer hindered by unsurmountable limitations to his knowledge and his power. This attitude creates itself a symbol, a new myth as it were, in the doctrine of the infinity of the world.

It can be demonstrated in the history of the human mind that the doctrine of the infinity of space was consciously understood as a transfer to the world of qualities which heretofore had been reserved to God. Nicolaus Cusanus thought the world infinite in space because he saw in it the intelligible image of God's absolute infinity which passes our understanding. Giordano Bruno, second to profess the infinity of the world, was a pantheist. Even Newton's sober physics still have a theological background at this point: Newton suffered his disciples to defend the doctrine that his absolute, infinite space was the sensorium of God. As modern times abandon religious thought, that connection sinks into the unconscious. But it is there nonetheless, I believe, and we shall take some pains to seek it out.

With the transition from the Middle Ages to modern times, the emphasis in the thought and life of man is clearly moving away from God, toward the world. But now the world consists in the duality of man and nature. Behind this duality there is concealed the more abstract and probably even more fundamental contrast between subject and object. In the concluding chapter I may perhaps be permitted a guess why this contrast emerged at this precise moment in history. But it is certain that the Middle Ages did not know the contrast in such sharpness. For in the Christian world-view God is always there as third and most important agent beside man and nature. And God combines within himself, raised to the highest degree, those two principles that we today should call subjectivity and objectivity: the *ens realissimum* is at once the personal God. In modern times, man and nature divide among themselves God's infinity, no less than his other attributes.

Within himself, man realizes the boundless riches of his own soul, outside himself he witnesses the dissolution of the barriers to his freedom and power. Even within the Christian religion, the religious process is transferred inside the individual by late medieval mysticism, the Reformation, and pietism. In the secular sphere, the humanist liberation of man brings with it the great subjective art; the rational liberation brings science and enlightenment; political liberation produces the state emancipated from the church, and democracy; technical liberation results in wilful transformation of the face of the earth. But man, boundlessly free and powerful, would be without sustenance if he were not sure that he is dealing with something which has objective existence. For those who want knowledge, there is waiting in nature the infinite treasure of truth, for those who want action, the infinite field of action. Some modern men have loved nature with that infinite love that once belonged to God and God alone. But for all modern men, nature has been the setting in which alone human life was secure. Therefore, nature had to be immutably real, and without limits, else she would not have offered firm support to the subject who is endlessly reaching out beyond himself.

These general reflections are borne out by the specific inquiry in which we are here engaged, the inquiry into the history of nature. The doctrine of the infinity of time means, to begin with, the abandonment of the essentially historic thinking of Christianity. The history of salvation can now no longer be the sole content of the course of the world, and nature seems ahistoric. In the nineteenth century, the idea of the historic character of nature begins to take hold through the theory of evolution. This theory soon achieves almost religious dignity. As the history of salvation did once, so now infinite upward evolution endows all life with meaning. But since nature has now taken the place of God, history is no longer a drama enacted between God and the world, but a process that carries its power and justification within itself. Man no longer hopes for transcendent grace, therefore he must face nature with optimism, or else despair. To what extent the success of the scientific world-view is due to its mythical content, is shown by a comparison of the theory of evolution with the Second Law of thermodynamics. Both were put forward around the middle of the nineteenth century as purely scientific theories. The theory of evolution quickly became the battle cry of every modern mind. The Second Law, on the other hand, remained a technical detail of physics; subterfuge was used to evade its application to the world as a whole. For the prospect of the heat death of the world, however far off in the future, would have shaken the faith that life has meaning.

In later chapters I shall show that both the theory of evolution and the Second Law are closely related consequences of the historic character of the world. But for the moment I shall defer this purely scientific consideration, and discuss the intellectual and spiritual situation that is reflected in our present-day ideas of infinity.

The doubts raised at the outset of this chapter about the infinity of space and time could still be considered as merely hypothetical doubts. Even so, I fail to see how we can escape the conclusion that, according to the Second Law, each portion of the world possesses only a finite reserve of events. What is more, the mere appearance of such hypotheses in itself betrays already a new mode of thought, and this is what concerns us here. In many other branches of natural science, this mode of thought has already worked out for itself conceptual systems that are well developed and empirically well founded. The special theory of relativity has set an upper limit for possible speeds, the quantum theory a lower limit for the application of our entire spatio-causal model of the world. Even mathematics, compelled by paradoxes, is attempting to supplant or to justify concepts of infinity by those of probability.

What is the hallmark of this mode of thought? If I

may use the catchword for once, it is its pragmatism. We are no longer convinced that we may apply a concept unhesitatingly in areas where there is no possibility to test our right to apply it. To be sure, this has been a guiding principle of modern science ever since Galileo. But we are finding out today that in some respects we have never really applied the principle. True, there are in our surroundings, and a good stretch beyond them, things that exist as such within the space and time of our intuition, and that require nothing but discovery. But as we try to penetrate to the last foundations of nature in the infinitely small, or to her outermost borders in the infinitely distant, we grow aware that our plain, clear picture of the world was only an aspect of the immediate foreground. In those remotest reaches of nature, only that is still comprehensible to us which is of our making or which, at least, could be of our making. It has become clearer than ever before that knowledge and power belong together. We have to give up forming concepts about objects which cannot become the objects of a subject, at least in principle. Pragmatic science has the view of nature that is fitting for a technical age.

Why is it that this step had not been taken before at some time since the beginning of the modern age? It is true that the experiences that forced the step were made only lately. But there are other reasons why before it had not even been considered, and why it meets even today with the most ardent resistance particularly among many natural scientists. The idea of infinite nature existing as such, this idea that we have to give up, is the myth of modern science. Science has started out by destroying the

myth of the Middle Ages. And now science is forced by
its own consistency to realize that it has merely raised another myth instead. If man lets go of this myth too, what
hold is left to him?

We must leave no room here for groundless hopes.
Those who have understood that the myth of the natural
sciences, the myth of the object, was merely a substitute
symbolism, may greet its decay as a liberation. But this
step is still purely negative. I do not think that it reopens
the way back to the older myths of religion. For we have
given up the myths of science not because they are science,
but because they are myths. I do believe, however, that
the answers to the problems we are now facing must be
sought in the sphere of religion. But these answers will no
longer be of any use to us if they are expressed in terms
of myth. The great parables alone will no longer do.
More insistently than former times we must ask for the
essence itself.

The question for the essence begins with the realization
that we are face to face with nothingness. Free, knowing
man is master of his objects, and for this very reason they
lend him no support. One glance at today's physical technology tells us this much. It will become still clearer once
we have succeeded in forcing the spheres of life and of the
soul also more completely under the rule of objectifying
knowledge. Everything lies within our power, including
self-destruction. No authority tells us any longer how to
use the power. Nothing justifies the hope that power of
its own accord will work for the good. If today's science,
unmythical though it has become, is itself still a symbol,
it is a symbol, first of all, of this nothingness.

The attitude that grows out of the experience of nothingness is today often called nihilism. The meaning of this word is of such importance that we dare not mistake it.

There have always been men who know only their own advantage. For them the problem that troubles us here does not exist, since they consider meaningful whatever profits them. But at all times the world of man has lasted only because there were others who felt compelled to ask for the meaning of the whole, and to act out of a sense of responsibility for the whole. What I want to call nihilism is not the baseness of the first but the objective desperation of the second sort of man. This desperation takes on different forms, and has different effects, according to the degree of honesty with which it faces its own situation.

There is an honest nihilism, the confession that hopes are not worth holding, that values have collapsed, that life is without meaning. This is among the most honest positions man can take today. But it is hardly possible to take it and go on living.

Then there is cynical nihilism. Deep down it is aware of the senselessness of its existence, but it refrains from applying the awareness to its own appetites. It lets itself be drawn into the game for power, since its own wickedness and the agonies of others are no more real to it than are happiness, faith, or love.

Finally there is illusionary nihilism. Unable to bear the despair of honesty or the playfulness of cynicism, it seizes on the first value, ideal, or hope that comes along, and tells itself that it has found meaning and salvation.

This is the nihilism of the flight from truth. It does not know that it destroys its values precisely by making on them demands they cannot meet.

I am not speaking here of nihilism at such length because I believe it to be the final answer. But there is no escape, I fear, from its illusionary form unless we open our minds to its honest form. Nihilism is the question for the essence itself, the question that concerns us. Please hold on to this question.

The answer I should like to offer can be formulated only at the end of this work. Here I want to add merely that nihilism seems to me to be the negative counterpole of Christianity. We shall not understand one pole without the other.

VI

Star Systems

FROM the remotest reaches of cosmic history, past the many stages in the growth of forms, we shall attempt now to find our way back to where we as human beings of today are standing. The heavens brought forth the earth, on earth life grew, within life stirs the soul, and in man the soul becomes conscious of itself. This is the outline—how shall we give it content? We have hardly the time to retell individual historical sequences of events. What we must search for are the motive forces of history. The movement of history is given. Can we understand if it was necessary, or even how it was at all possible?

This chapter and the next are devoted to the history of the heavens up to the origin of the earth. Here, I shall illustrate some of the theories about the motive forces of cosmic history in general. The next chapter will deal with the particular problems of the evolution of the stars.

What may the beginning of the history of the heavens have been like? In the third and fourth chapters I have presented the empirical information on which we can rely. One of the possible hypotheses, covering all of this information, is the following:

Some billions of years ago, all the matter that is now

contained in the portion of the world we know, was compressed into a narrow space. At that time the heavy elements came into being out of light atomic nuclei, possibly hydrogen nuclei. Then matter flew apart and scattered through space in the form of a more and more diffuse gas. I shall not speculate on what may have preceded the original state of compression, or whether it lasted a long while or only an instant.

This, I believe, is the most probable view at present. In any event, it is the most conservative among the views we can adopt today, since it covers our experiences without postulating new laws of nature. Still, we are not able to refute, in its most general terms, the following view advanced by Pascal Jordan: During the expansion of already existing matter, new matter constantly came into being. The moment when the expansion started is also the moment when no matter at all was as yet in existence. According to this view, the world would arise in continuity out of nothing.

I shall leave these questions open, and turn to a subject with which we can deal at a high degree of probability within the framework of the known laws of nature. That is the evolution of the great star systems, especially the extra-galactic nebulae.

I must first briefly discuss method. The question what the motive forces are is the crowning question, but for that very reason it is not the first one that an inquiry into the history of evolution has to ask. First we must know the existing forms exactly: morphology is always the beginning. Next we must know the time sequence of the forms, in the order of their origin: the second step, therefore, is empirical genetics. This could also be termed morphology in point of time, since it teaches us to understand development as temporal form. Only now do we possess the material that we want to explain: causal analysis is the third step. But to explain a process causally means in contemporary physics no longer to reduce it to pressure, or thrust, or any other mechanical process that seems to be immediately intelligible. Causal explanation is the connection of events by mathematical laws of nature. Mathematics, in turn, is nothing else than the study of the most general possible structures, whether they exist in space, or in time, or merely in pure concept. A law of nature we call a structure of events that under certain given conditions appears always and everywhere. Hence, our method of advancing from morphology to genetics and on to causal analysis means that we are learning to distinguish structural relations which are less and less within the realm of sense perception, and therefore are more and more generally valid. With reference to the single event, our method means the recognition of the essential likeness of this event to many other events already known. With reference to the search for last principles, it means an increase in our store of immediate, though thoroughly tested intuition, and we need this store to ask the largest questions.

The three steps of our method are separated more sharply in concept than in practice. We often do not begin to see the essence of a form until we study its origin. And we often do not know the temporal sequence of forms, and discover it only as we study the laws by which they must have arisen. This is our position particularly with regard to the celestial bodies, since they show hardly ever any change during our short lifetime, and since the one and only document their past has left us is their present form.

Let us study the pictures of a few star systems (opp. p. 90).

The first picture shows a group of distant nebulae. The single stars scattered over the picture are parts of our Milky Way system. They are the foreground beyond which we see the nebulae.

The picture shows three nebulae grouped near its center. Two of them show the beginnings of a spiral structure, while the third one, most nearly in the center of the picture, is perfectly round and most likely globular in shape. Each of them has in reality a lengthwise diameter of tens of thousands of light-years.

Pictures two and three show two spiral nebulae, one seen from its axis, the other from its edge. Either has at its center a dense core, approaching spherical shape. Spiral arms, forming a very flat disk of loosely distributed matter, are joined to the outside of the core. Core and arms consist of stars. But the arms also contain matter in the form of gas and dust. In picture three the dust can be noticed since it absorbs light where it is between us and the core. The form of these nebulae is fairly regular in its large outline, but in detail it is irregularly cloudy.

Picture four shows the Great Cloud of Magellan, a nebula that displays irregular cloud shape even in its outline.

Picture five shows a globular star cluster. With it we have left the realm of the great extra-galactic nebulae. A large nebula contains ten billion to a hundred billion stars, a globular star cluster only about a hundred thousand. The cluster here shown follows our Milky Way, it is one of the perhaps two hundred such clusters that surround our system in loose arrangement. Some of the extra-galactic systems, the Andromeda nebula for instance, are likewise surrounded by globular clusters. These clusters are by no means spheres with a firmly defined surface. They possess only the symmetry of a sphere, but their density of stars, like that of the large nebulae, fades imperceptibly into empty space. Morphologically, they are a counterpart to the irregular nebulae like Magellan's Cloud. They possess not only the well-defined spherical symmetry, but their interior, too, is without cloudy irregularities in its density of stars, and free of gas or dust.

Finally, there are two pictures of gaseous nebulae within the Milky Way. Picture six shows the famous Orion nebula, visible to the naked eye in the "sword buckle" of Orion as the center star of the three that can be seen there one above the other. Picture seven, too, shows nebular masses in the constellation of Orion. These nebulae are far smaller than the globular clusters. They are several hundred light-years away from us, and may contain enough matter to form ten or a hundred stars. They are gaseous, in part probably mingled with dust. They shine only if illumined by stars. If a star stands behind them they absorb part of its light. They are shown here to give an impression of the state of free, so-called inter-stellar masses of gas within the star systems.

After we have observed the forms, we attempt to classify them morphologically. I maintain that all celestial objects may be assigned to one of three classes: clouds, rotatory forms, and spheres. Pictures four, six, and seven show clouds, pictures two and three rotatory figures, picture five a sphere. To demonstrate that all other stars fit into the same classes is more than my space allows.

Clouds have irregular outlines and an equally irregular internal structure. A cloud generally consists of smaller clouds. The comparison with the clouds in our atmosphere covers the essential features. With a somewhat broadminded definition, I should like to call rotatory figures all those formations which show that their shape has something to do with rotation. Most of them have a well-defined plane and, vertical to the plane, a well-defined axis. They flatten out into that plane, and often possess a pronounced central mass. The planetary system of our own sun, for instance, is a rotatory figure in the meaning of my definition. Some rotatory figures, such as the spiral nebulae for example, have an internally cloudy structure, others do not. The spheres, as I said earlier, do not necessarily have a definite surface, but may have spherical symmetry only. Their interior is not cloudy.

What may be the genetic relation among these classes? All three types are found among the large star systems as well as among the masses in the order of magnitude of a single star. It would seem, therefore, that the size of a system does not determine its type. The supposition suggests itself that the type is a symptom of the age of the individual system. If this is true, then every system would in the course of its evolution pass through all three types. In what sequence, and for what reasons?

To simplify our reflections, I shall begin with a hypothesis that will have to prove itself by its success. It is the same hypothesis that has nearly always been made in speculations on the origin of the stars. I shall assume that all stars and star systems have been formed out of diffuse masses of gas. If this assumption is correct, we should gain an idea of the earliest state of the stars by looking at the gaseous masses still in existence today. Let us look once more at pictures six and seven. They show chaotic fluctuation. This, then, would be the initial state of matter. The cloud form would be closest to the origin, it would be the youngest form.

That the original state was gaseous we shall assume. That it then must have had cloud shape I shall develop from that assumption. Evidently, these gasses are in internal commotion. In the condition in which we see them they could not even remain at rest, since the pressure of gas tends to equalize its differences in density. Their form of motion is called turbulent. The cloud shape is the visible picture of turbulent motion. An exact definition of turbulent motion is the following: Turbulence is that form of motion in which supplementary currents, changing irregularly from place to place and from moment to moment, are superimposed on the general main current. The flow of a gas or a liquid that is not turbulent is called laminar. In other words, laminar motion is that in which all particles flow uniformly, and neighboring particles flow along similar paths—in short, an orderly movement. The flow of hot asphalt from the tipped-over barrel, the flow of honey from the spoon are laminar. Turbulent is the motion of almost all large masses of gas or liquid. Look into a flowing river, into the dance of the snowflakes, or into the clouds in the sky, and you will see turbulence. Theoretical considerations allow us to understand the reasons for this predominance of turbulence.

Turbulence is a phenomenon of disorder. It brings to mind the Second Law of thermodynamics. Apparently, turbulence has nothing to do with the strict thermodynamic formulation of the Second Law, but it follows directly from its statistical extension. Let us suppose two masses of gas are flowing past each other in laminar motion. Minimal divergences from that motion, such as can always occur, will cause particles from both masses to intermingle. This will increase the disorder, more particles will mingle, and this will go on until the motion has become turbulent throughout. We do not know in detail how this process occurs. Nor do we need to know it—probably it is different in every single instance. We conclude statistically, as in the Second Law. Laminar motion is a macro-state of low statistical probability, since here the movement of the whole determines the movement of all the parts. If laminar motion changes somehow in a small detail, it soon turns into some form of turbulence. But if turbulence changes in some small detail, it turns with overwhelming probability only into some other form of turbulence. Laminar motion turns into turbulent motion just because in that transformation an amount of energy is transferred from ordered to disordered motion in the meaning of the Second Law. Hence, turbulence is more probable than laminarity, but it is not the most probable state of energy possible. In turbulence, certain small areas of the gas still retain uniform motion. These areas are the smaller, the lower the viscosity of the moving matter. Still far more probable than turbulence is the state of heat in which each single atom follows its own path. Thus laminarity turns into turbulence, turbulence into heat. Turbulence is the intermediate state that leads the gas or liquid from ordered motion to heat death. The rivers and the winds on earth are still flowing only because the radiation of the sun constantly feeds them with new energy. In the universe, the turbulent motion of smaller masses of gas such as the Orion nebula is most likely being fed by the internal motion of the large system—in this case, of the Milky Way. But as far as we can determine, the large system does not have further external sources of kinetic energy. In time its motion must die, and the motion of all its gaseous partial systems must die with it. It is my opinion, now, that the road to this extinction leads through the rotatory figures, and often beyond them to the spheres.

To begin with, we must search for the causes of the individuality of the varous systems. Clouds separate and combine again. They have no lasting individuality. Why did the diffuse matter in the universe combine into separate nebulae, and why did separate stars develop in the nebulae? The cause is gravitation, the mutual attraction of all matter. To be sure, in an infinite mass of gas of uniform density, every single point would be attracted by its surroundings with equal force in all directions, and so it would remain at rest. But if perchance the matter at some point is somewhat denser than around that point, it will attract its surroundings with an extra margin of force. In this way it can attract more matter, its density increases further, and an individual system may come into existence. I shall pass over the details of the conditions under which this might occur.

Ever since the initial explosion, now, matter is in motion, and no doubt soon in turbulent motion. This offers ample occasion for chance concentrations of matter. Once such concentrations have been formed for some time and have expended by radiation the energy that had become available in their formation, it would be difficult to dissolve them again. For energy would now be required to separate their parts.

A partial system forming within a turbulent cloud will as a rule rotate from the beginning. Only by chance could the disordered partial motions balance each other in such a way that no rotation would occur. If, for instance, a system is formed out of two main masses that have come close to one another by chance, it is likely that the two masses have not met exactly head-on, but have run a little aslant of one another. If now they hook on to each other because of mutual attraction, and finally combine into a single mass, they will be drawn into a spin due to the lateral component of their motion, just like two dancers or acrobats who run past each other and, at the moment of closest approach, catch each other's arm. This is only an example—almost all complicated cases would be similar.

According to the mechanical law of the preservation of rotatory momentum, a body so formed does not loose its spinning motion. Therefore, if the internal turbulent motions of the body decrease, it will assume the shape of a flattened rotatory figure. This, I believe, is the stage reached by the spiral nebulae. I suppose that their spiral form, too, can be explained by the combined effect of turbulence and rotation. The turbulence which still exists, and which is constantly stimulated anew by the rotation, leads again and again to the formation of clouds. The clouds in turn are again and again spooled up in the rotation, in the form of spirals. For matter near the center rotates more rapidly than near the edges. This fact is established empirically and is quite plausible intuitively. But since it is important for what follows I shall also prove it. The cohesion among the nebula particles is far too loose for the entire nebulae to rotate like a solid body, like a flying disk for example. Rather, the shape of the nebula is maintained by the fact that the two main forces—gravitation pulling inward, centrifugal force drawing outward—hold each other in balance at every point. The centrifugal force is a consequence of rotation. Gravitation, now, is stronger near the center than toward the edges. Consequently, the centrifugal force too must be stronger near the center, or in other words, matter near the center must rotate faster than matter at some distance from the center. In this way, the clouds would be drawn out more and more into spiral form, and would finally be wrapped around the core of the nebula like thread around a spool. But turbulence does not allow events to reach that point. After a time, turbulence destroys its own handiwork. New clouds arise, and the spooling up begins all over. This explains the regularity in general, and the variety in detail, that are the distinctive features of the spiral nebulae.

But the lack of uniformity of rotation will finally destroy rotation. New turbulence arises constantly. It drains rotation constantly of energy, energy that in the end is constantly converted into heat. The heat, in turn, is radiated away into space. And so rotation must finally cease. This seems to contradict the law of the preservation of rotary momentum. But the seeming contradiction disappears when we take a closer look at the mechanism that causes rotation to cease. The turbulent fluctuation of the mass has an equalizing effect on its rotation, just as though the gas were very viscous. Quickly rotating masses near the center move toward the edges and there speed up rotation, while slowly rotating masses move toward the center and there slow rotation down. This process constantly upsets the balance in both regions between gravitation and centrifugal force. Near the center, rotation is now too slow, gravitation predominates, and the masses sink slowly into the core. Outside, rotation is too fast, centrifugal force predominates, and the masses escape into the void. The core remains behind, rotating weakly, the rotatory momentum had escaped with the outside masses. They swarm through space once more and finally combine with other masses into a new system.

I am inclined to the view that the globular systems originated in this fashion—that they are such cores which have remained behind. The spheres then would be the oldest systems, as the clouds are the youngest. The terms "old" and "young" are used here not primarily in terms of years but relative to the tempo of evolution of the system itself. Large systems evolve more slowly than small ones. Thus, if a large and a small system are of the same age in terms of years, the smaller one will show a more advanced stage of evolution. This is in harmony with the fact that comparatively small isolated systems, such as globular star clusters, are of the oldest type, while very large nebulae like our Milky Way are of the rotatory type that is still cloudy inside. We are able to estimate that a globular cluster will lose its rotation in approximately one hundred million years, but the Milky Way only in over five billion years. Thus, the Milky Way is still rotating because the world has not existed long enough for its rotation to cease.

One reservation must be made here, however. Our reflections assume that the systems consist of diffuse gas. Once stars have formed within a system, the transfer of energy from one point to another is slower, hence the loss of rotation is slower. A system composed exclusively of stars can go on rotating for a very long time. The planets, for instance, are still revolving around the sun. Certain extra-galactic nebulae of the so-called elliptical type seem to be in a similar condition. I lack the space to give details.

I want to close this chapter with a fundamental consideration. The path from clouds to rotatory figures and on to spheres is a path from disorder to order, from chaos to form. Is not this contradicting the Second Law?

It cannot contradict the Second Law, since nowhere in my reflections have I assumed any physically impossible process. But it will be instructive to study why there is no contradiction. I shall proceed in two steps. First, I shall merely clear up the seeming contradiction. Second, I shall show that the evolution of forms of which I have just given an example is in reality a necessary consequence of the historic character of the universe.

Visible form is not the only kind of order. Gaseous

matter that is originally in motion contains much kinetic energy which in the end is converted into heat. The gain in thermodynamic probability of the state brought about by this conversion is so immense that the small loss of probability connected with the formation of regular forms is negligible by comparison. This point, too, I should like to make clear with a quaint illustration. Imagine a plain, and on it a hill with a fairly smooth top. On the hill-top, there is a large number of well-polished wooden balls. A slight push, and the balls are set rolling. They roll in all directions down to the foot of the hill and then some distance until they come to a standstill. If the territory is not too irregular they will now form a circle around the hill. Anyone seeing this formation will consider it extremely improbable. The circle strikes us as a higher, more specific degree of order than the original state in which all the balls were heaped on top of the hill. Actually the original condition is statistically more improbable, for then the wooden balls, beside their geometrical order, also possessed the potential energy of their elevated position, the energy that enabled them later to roll into the form of the circle. Had the balls originally been scattered over the plain where only the winds and the rabbits played with them, it might be conceivable that by chance they would have come to form a circle around the hill. But it could never have happened that even one single ball reached the hill-top by itself.

Hence, whenever we apply the concept of order in the meaning of the Second Law, we must look out for the relations of energy.

This negative argument, however, does not suffice.

We have seen that the origin of forms does not necessarily contradict the Second Law. But are we able to understand that forms arise of necessity?

What is a form in the meaning of this question? I shall understand form to mean a formation of matter which, by its spatial and physical properties, is clearly set off from its surroundings. A spiral nebula, a uranium mineral, a hermit crab, or a sign on the blackboard are forms. For the moment I shall call form only the single material thing itself, and not the abstract quality "form" that all things of the same form have in common. Of two forms of nearly the same size we shall call more differentiated the one in which we can distinguish the larger number of different individual forms. A house inhabited by men is more differentiated than an erratic rock, and the rock is more differentiated than a cubic foot of inter-stellar gas. We assume as a convincing law of experience that forms can come only out of such other forms whose degree of differentiation is not too much different from their own. Differentiated forms do not come to be "by themselves." We might call this the principle of continuity in the origin of forms. It is the reason why forms are the best documents of the past: they are factors whose mere existence allows us to draw many conclusions about the factual events of the past. That we cannot in the same manner draw conclusions from present shapes about the future, is due to the statistical formulation of the Second Law. A form is an improbable state because it is a kind of order. The Second Law allows us to conclude from the existence of the form that something still more improbable has existed in the past, an energy, namely, capable of producing this form. But about the future we can predict merely that there will be something more probable. Dissolution of the form in any way, or even its unchanged continuance accompanied by irreversible changes in its surroundings, will bring about a more probable state. Thus, the conclusion into the future lacks all precision. Even inanimate nature, in an objective and unconscious way, has a memory for the past but nothing analogous for the future.

How do these ideas advance our present inquiry? Nature creates forms and destroys them. The number of forms of a certain degree of differentiation remains constant if an equal number of them come to be and perish at any one time. For instance, there is always approximately the same number of waves in the ocean, and approximately the same total number of plants and animals on earth. Origin and decay usually occur at separate points. Not every form that perishes creates a new one, rather one form perishes here while somewhere else another one of more or less the same order comes into existence. The equilibrium exists only in the average. This equilibrium is disturbed when either origin or decay predominates. Decay may prevail when there are large-scale events destroying forms. Origin may prevail, for instance, when individuals of a certain form are coming into existence but do not yet exist in large numbers—for in this case those that could perish do not yet exist. For the number of forms that perish is usually proportionate to the number in existence, while the number of forms that originate often is not.

Such a prevalence of origin seems to me to be the case

PLATE 1

A GROUP OF DISTANT NEBULAE

PLATE 2

Spiral Nebula, Center View

PLATE 3

Spiral Nebula, Edge View

PLATE 4

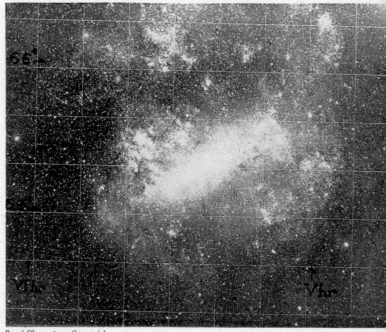

Royal Observatory, Greenwich

THE GREAT CLOUD OF MAGELLAN

PLATE 5

unt Wilson Observatory

GREAT GLOBULAR STAR CLUSTER IN HERCULES

PLATE 6

Yerkes Observatory

GREAT GASEOUS NEBULA IN ORION

PLATE 7

ORION, THE GREAT CURVED NEBULA

PLATE 8

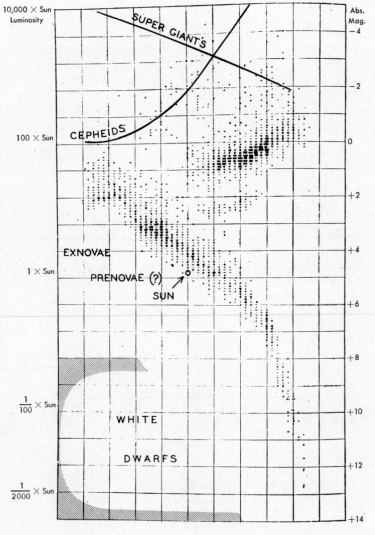

10,000 × Sun Luminosity

SUPER GIANTS

100 × Sun

CEPHEIDS

EXNOVAE

1 × Sun

PRENOVAE (?)

SUN

WHITE

DWARFS

1/100 × Sun

1/2000 × Sun

Abs. Mag.

−4

−2

0

+2

+4

+6

+8

+10

+12

+14

RUSSELL-HERTZSPRUNG DIAGRAM. (Adapted from Skilling and Richardson, *Astronomy*, by permission of Henry Holt & Co.)

in the history of the celestial bodies. The chaotic original fog we have assumed is very poor in differentiated, lasting forms. But it is rich in energy. Many events may come out of it, and gradually these events will bring about forms. Why the beginning is poor in forms we do not know. But man has always been inclined to imagine the beginning in that fashion, and experience supports his inclination. We are encountering a new trait of the historic character of the world. "The earth was void and empty, and the spirit of God moved over the waters." We are voicing the same truth when we say that in the beginning the earth was rich in potential but poor in actual form, rich in creative possibilities, poor in created structure. In time, there comes for every form the moment when origin and decay balance each other; it comes later, to be sure, in proportion as the forms are more differentiated. For a form can begin to originate only when another one, only slightly less differentiated, does already exist. We shall return to this point when we discuss the theory of evolution of life on earth.

The end always is heat death. Most of the time, however, it consists not in a dissolution of forms, but rather in their hardening. From the moment on when no more energy is converted, forms can neither originate nor decay. If I may be allowed for a moment, and only in the interest of simple expression, to call "life" any event affecting forms that contains a conversion of energy, the following statements are valid: Only death by external force destroys the form. Internal death does not tear the form down but leaves it behind. Death produces nothing but a corpse. Decomposition is already a sign of new life, though of a lower order. All life in the universe, on a scale large or small, is the evolution of forms of ever greater differentiation, enclosed between the original chaos and the hardening of the end.

These general reflections are reaching ahead of my subject. I must develop the history of forms step by step in the chapters that follow.

VII

Stars

DOWN from the great star systems, composed of
billions of luminous stars, we descend the scale of
magnitudes until we reach the single star. What do we
know of the evolution of fixed stars? What in particular
do we know of the star which is of the most immediate
concern to us, the sun with its system of planets?

As we study the stars, we find that even the way to
their morphology is paved with many indirect conclusions. Even in the best of our telescopes single stars show
as mere points of light. Their forms we cannot distinguish.
But even so we have been able over the last few decades
to develop a good system of classifying fixed stars according to their physical characteristics. The most important
features that we use in our classification are the star's absolute size, and its spectral type.

We must review here the significance of this classification. Let us look at the customary visual representation
of the existing star types, the so-called Russell-Hertzsprung diagram (facing p. 91).

Every point in this diagram signifies a possible type of
star. The type is indicated by two characteristics, shown

as the two coordinates of the diagram, either of which may vary along a continuous scale of values.

True brightness, in the meaning of the term as used in the third chapter, is indicated vertically, increasing from the bottom to the top of the diagram. True brightness is measured by so-called classes of absolute magnitude. In former times, stars were classified by their apparent brightness in six magnitudes—the expression "a star of the first magnitude" is still in common usage. Later, this rough classification was converted into a quantitative measure of brightness: two stars differ in brightness by exactly one magnitude when the brighter one is two and one half times as bright as the dimmer star. A low number of magnitude in this scale indicates great brightness. A difference of five magnitudes indicates that the brighter star is one hundred times brighter than the other. Absolute magnitude is the magnitude the star would have if it were located at a conventional standard distance, which has been set at thirty-three light-years. For instance, the sun has the absolute magnitude *five*, the stars of the greatest absolute brightness, shown in the upper part of the diagram, have approximately the absolute magnitude *minus five*—in other words, they are ten magnitudes or about ten thousand times brighter than the sun.

The spectral star types are indicated on the horizontal coordinate, from left to right. Stars are classified according to the lines that appear in the spectral dispersion of their light. We know today that differences in the spectra of various stars are due mainly to differences in their surface temperatures. In our diagram, the hotter stars are on the left, the cooler ones on the right. The diagram may also be read as showing the stars in the order of their color—hot stars are white, cool stars are red. The coolest stars that are still visible, those on the extreme right, have surface temperatures of around 3000° centigrade or 5300° Fahrenheit. The hottest stars reach 30,000° centigrade and more. We must remember that these high temperature figures have a precise physical meaning. Temperature is a measure of the average kinetic energy of atoms in heat motion. At a temperature of 30,000°, every atom has on the average ten times as much energy as at a temperature of 3000°.

The dots and crosses in the diagram indicate those combinations of both characteristics that are found in actual stars. Let us study first the densely dotted strip running from the upper left to the lower right. It is called the "main sequence." The vast majority of stars belong to this sequence, among them for example the well-known Sirius or dog star, Alpha Centauri, and our sun. The true brightness of the stars of the main sequence also indicates their surface temperature, and vice versa—the hotter a star, the brighter it is. We have a theory about the inner structure of the main sequence stars explaining this relation. I shall indicate its main points.

The matter composing the stars, due to its high temperature, is in a gaseous state. The inner portions of the star, being gaseous, must be considerably hotter than the surface, else they could not support the extreme pressure of the outer portions resting upon them. Since the inner portions are hotter than the surface, heat energy is constantly streaming from the inside to the outside by way of radiation. What we see as the surface of the star is the area where this stream of radiation gains free exit into the universe. On the basis of these two factors—the balance of pressure, and the constancy of the stream of radiation—we can compute the physical condition of the star. The result is that all the stars of the main sequence must have approximately the same center temperature, about twenty million degrees centigrade, thirty-five million degrees Fahrenheit. What distinguishes the various types of main sequence stars from one another is the amount of matter they contain. We can determine the amount of matter empirically in those instances where a star has a close companion. The motions that the two components of such a star, called binary or double star, describe around each other indicate their mutual attraction and thereby their masses. The faintest stars have about one quarter the mass of the sun, the brightest ones thirty times its mass. The larger the mass of a star, the greater is the stream of radiation issuing from it—in other words, the greater is the star's true brightness. If we now compare two stars of different mass, according to our theory their surface areas must differ less than their true brightness. This explains why the stream of radiation creates a greater density of heat energy, that is, a higher surface temperature, on a bright star than on a weaker one. These few remarks may suffice to indicate the connection between brightness and surface temperature of stars of the main sequence.

We now come to the question of the source of that stream of radiation continuously issuing from the stars. For the stars of the main sequence, we have an answer to this question too. At just about the temperature of thirty-five million degrees Fahrenheit, certain energy-producing reactions begin to take place in the atomic nuclei. At this temperature hydrogen changes into helium, with carbon and nitrogen acting as catalysts. This process is sufficient to maintain the present radiation of the sun for longer than one hundred billion years. Hence, the heat death of the universe is not yet just around the corner. If the sun in the course of its evolution has produced out of hydrogen all of the helium it contains today, it might conceivably have been shining for not quite one hundred billion years in the past. If the sun contained helium from the start, which seems likely, it might be any number of years younger.

What I am here recounting may perhaps seem highly speculative. How can we know what goes on in the innermost core of a star so far away that its surface appears as a mere point? In one short chapter, and without the aid of mathematics, I cannot produce the countless, carefully fashioned pieces of evidence that have gone into building our present astrophysical theories. I shall select two questions only: How do we know the chemical composition of the stars? And how certain are our conclusions about the center temperatures of the stars?

The chemical composition of the stars is determined with the aid of their spectra. Every element emits its characteristic spectral lines—as is well known, the presence of the rare gas helium was discovered on the sun before it was found on earth. Since even the most distant stars emit the same spectral lines as the elements on earth, the stars are obviously composed of the same substances as the earth. In point of quantity, however, light gasses and mainly hydrogen predominate greatly on the stars and in interstellar matter.

It is more difficult to determine the composition of the deep interior of the stars. But the theory I have just outlined indicates that the strength of the stream of radiation issuing from the main sequence stars cannot be understood quantitatively unless we assume the presence of much hydrogen in the interior of the stars also.

The center temperature of thirty-five million degrees has been determined at first only on the basis of pressure and stream of radiation. The result rested on the laws of classical physics and otherwise only on the well-known physics of the atomic shell. Then nuclear physics developed to the point where it was capable of stating deductively the possible nuclear reactions within the star. We are, of course, unable to maintain on earth a temperature of thirty-five million degrees Fahrenheit. But we have electrical equipment with whose aid we can impart to single atomic nuclei energies far in excess of those they would have at thirty-five million degrees. This temperature corresponds to a tension of about one hundred thousand volts in the laboratory, while we can produce millions of volts. Thus we know from the laboratory the behavior of atomic nuclei in every one of the reactions that, as we claim, occur in the interior of the stars. If we calculate, with the help of these data, at what temperature the reactions would occur in such a way that they would furnish just the right energy of radiation, the result is precisely thirty-five million degrees Fahrenheit. This complete harmony between the result found by nuclear physics and the result found earlier by an entirely different method argues strongly for the truth of both theories. We interpret the harmony in physical terms by saying that in the center of the star exactly that temperature will prevail at which the supply of energy, and the loss of energy through radiation, balance each other. This balance regulates itself. If, for instance, the supply of energy were for a moment too small, then the region around the center of the star could no longer support the pressure from the outside portions. It would be compressed further, and thereby its temperature would be raised. The processes in the center, being highly sensitive to temperature, would be accelerated by the increase in heat to such a degree that the balance of energy supply would be restored.

We are not yet able to tell exactly how the stars came into existence. We can state, however, that certain stars of the main sequence, the brightest ones, must be young. This means to say that the matter they contain today cannot have been combined in them for more than ten to one hundred million years. The "germ" of the stars may be older. This conclusion, too, is based on several independent considerations. The brightest stars of the main sequence are only about thirty times as heavy as the sun, but they are ten thousand times as bright. Consequently, they consume their energy-producing hydrogen three hundred times as fast. It is impossible that they have carried on this rate of consumption since the beginning of the world. Since they are here today, they cannot have been here a billion years ago. These stars, now, show in their spectra signs of very violent rotation. They would have to be counted among the rotatory figures, while most of the other stars are spheres. By this criterion, too, they are young. But we must not lose ourselves in these particulars. There is still a rich field for future research in this direction.

I also want to say a few words about the stars not in the main sequence.

First let us look at the stars below the main sequence, the so-called "white dwarfs." They are dwarfs, that is, their true brightness is low, but they are white, that is, their surface is very hot. The strength of radiation per square inch of a star's surface increases rapidly with the surface temperature. Since the white dwarfs in spite of their high temperatures shine but dimly, it follows that their surface must have fewer square inches than that of normal stars. In other words, geometrically they are small. But the amount of matter they contain is not small. The best known of them, the satellite of Sirius, has approximately the mass of the sun, but the diameter of the earth. In many cases the density of matter in white dwarfs exceeds the density of water a hundred thousand times. A cubic inch of such matter would weigh more than a ton and a half. But no cubic inch could be removed from the star without returning immediately into the normal state of matter—its condition is entirely the consequence of the extreme pressure on the star. This pressure is so great that it squashes some of the atomic shells.

If there were any hydrogen in the interior of these stars, some very violent nuclear reactions would have to occur because of this high density and temperature. These reactions in turn would produce a great deal of energy, and the star would have to shine more brightly than the stars of the main sequence. We must conclude from this that the white dwarfs contain no hydrogen. They are most likely old stars that have already consumed their hydrogen. If so, they would be an illustration of the incipient heat death of a star.

Above the main sequence, the diagram shows a large variety of star types. I shall discuss only the most frequent type, the yellow and red giants. They are giants, that is, their true brightness is great, and they are yellow and red, that is, their surface temperature is low. We draw exactly the opposite conclusion of what we said for the white dwarfs, namely, that the giants have a very large surface. Some of them are so large that if the sun were placed in their center, the earth, revolving at normal distance from the sun, would still be inside the giant. The red star at the upper left of Orion, called Betelgeuse, is of this type. And yet the mass of the yellow and red giants is barely larger than that of the sun. Their matter is greatly thinned out, in a condition which in terrestrial physics we should call a high vacuum. They may, however, contain a dense core similar to a white dwarf. If so, what we see would be merely a very extended atmosphere. Various criteria indicate that the giants are old. I shall not go into the details of their still highly hypothetical theory.

A passing mention must also be given to the new stars, the so-called novae, that often attract so much attention. They are stars that flare up into brilliant brightness within a few hours or days, only to grow as dim as before after a few weeks or months. They do not come newly into existence, their short prominence is due merely to a sudden violent burst of light. They are of two essentially different kinds, the ordinary novae and the super-novae. Among the innumerable theories about these outbursts I believe the following two are at present the most probable: Normal novae might be "heat lightning," or chains of events produced by the sudden upset of a thermically unstable stratification of the star's gasses, a stratification that might have been building up over long periods, perhaps thousands of years. The event would be similar to what we see on a smaller scale during hot summer days on earth. Super-novae are perhaps the events in which a rapidly rotating star tears in two, and a binary star comes into existence. But we can hardly interpret the abnormalities of an evolutionary process before we have fully understood the law of normal evolution.

Once again we shall narrow the field of our inquiry. We shall leave the fixed stars, and study the origin of the planetary system of our sun.

We begin again with morphology. The planetary system is among the most differentiated, one is tempted to say the most artful formations in the world of stars. The central body dominating the system is the sun. The sun weighs a thousand times as much as Jupiter, largest of the planets, and Jupiter alone weighs more than all the other planets put together. The planets revolve around the sun. All their orbits lie very exactly in one and the same plane. On this plane, the planets are describing paths that come very close to being perfect circles, and all revolve in the same direction. If the planets have moons, these moons too move on nearly the same plane and in the same direction. If the planets have a noticeable rotation around their own axis, it also goes in the same direction. There are among the outermost planets a few exceptions to the rules about moons and rotation, but they barely detract from the impression of an all-embracing order within the system. There is further a law governing the distance of the planets from the sun. For the outer planets, from Mars on out to Uranus, it can be stated as simply as this: Each planet is twice as far from the sun as the next closer one.

This structural order of the system is not merely a consequence of the laws of mechanics. According to Kepler's laws, to which Newton gave a mechanical explanation, every planet must run on a plane. But there is no necessity for all of these planes to coincide. Jupiter's plane could be at right angles with that of Saturn without violating a law of mechanics. Further, while the orbits of the planets must be ellipses, no mechanical law demands that they be almost circles. And, finally, no law of mechanics has to be satisfied by the distances of the various planets from the sun. All in all it can be said that there are over-riding laws governing the formation of the entire system, while under the laws of mechanics each planet could revolve in its own way and follow a course completely different from all the others.

These signs of order have in the past called forth much speculation about a supra-mechanical factor or over-seer, regulating the structure of the system. But the correct interpretation is probably that first given by Kant: The form of the system must be understood historically. It is a relic of the time when the planets were still physically interconnected. I shall immediately reformulate this assumption in the manner that seems to me the most accurate at the present state of our knowledge: When the sun was young, it probably rotated rapidly like all celestial bodies that develop out of turbulent masses of gas. Its rotation must have died down in the manner I described in the preceding chapter. A gaseous sphere remained behind, today's sun. The rotatory momentum of the system was carried outward by departing masses of gas. These gasses, for some time, must have formed something like a rotating disk around what today is the sun. The side view may perhaps have been similar to the nebula in picture three. Only, the diameter of that nebula is tens of thousands of light-years, that of the solar system a few light-hours. The present planets, now, are remnants of that disk. They have retained its form of motion. This is why they revolve in circles, all on the same plane, and all in the same direction. A closer study of the currents that had to develop in that rotating mass of gas seems to me to explain also why planets could develop only at certain regular distances from the sun.

But why are any remnants at all left of that mass of gas? Why did the gas not stream away completely? In order to understand this we must look at the chemical composition of the planets. Let us select the planet we know best, our earth. Its crust consists largely of silicates, that is, compounds of silicon and oxygen. Aluminum, magnesium, and iron are added, all of them elements heavier than hydrogen. We know today that these elements constitute less than the one hundreth part of the total mass of the sun, and of those fixed stars we have been able to analyze. In those stars the light gasses hydrogen and helium predominate by a wide margin. As far as we know, the composition of the inter-stellar gas is also like that of those stars. The planets, therefore, are chemically speaking an exception in the universe. They are accumulations of the small traces that exist of heavy elements. Accumulations of this sort, on a small scale, are also present elsewhere in the universe. Between the stars there is not only gas, there is also dust, that is, solid though very small particles of matter. This dust becomes noticeable when it occurs in clouds, because then it absorbs the light of the stars. It must consist of heavy elements, because light elements would not combine into solid particles—they remain gaseous even under the conditions prevailing in inter-stellar space. We can easily imagine how cosmic dust was formed. When atoms of heavy, condensable elements collide, they will often cling to one another, and in the end they will form small particles. Such particles may keep on growing due to further collisions. In the universe, where the particles are scattered very thinly, this process will take a very long time. But in the considerably denser masses of gas near the sun it could within a few million years lead to bodies of the size of planets. I am inclined to think that our own earth came to be in this fashion, by a gradual accumulation of small bits the size of dust particles, meteorites, and planetoids. And once a body of the size of the earth is formed, it no longer drifts along with every movement of the gas. The cloud of gas could now stream away while the system of solid bodies remained behind, just like the skeleton remains behind after the decomposition of a cadaver.

If this theory is true, there is no reason why our planetary system should be the only one in the world. We cannot see whether the fixed stars have planets, because of their great distances from the earth. But recently disturbances have been noticed in the motions of two fixed stars relatively close to us, and have been ascribed to the attraction of planet-like bodies. It therefore seems permissible to assume that planets are a frequent occurrence in the universe. And to the question we are bound to ask: "Is there life elsewhere in the universe?" we have at any rate no right to answer in the negative.

VIII

The Earth

IT IS generally assumed that in the beginning the earth was in a hot-liquid state, and that it has cooled off since. As I said earlier, I myself would prefer to think that the earth has been built up slowly out of smaller fragments. These fragments, however, were cold. For they were as far from the sun as the earth is today, and had no reason to be hotter than the surface of the earth. But there were reasons why the earth should warm up in the process of its formation, and it is certain that today the earth's interior has temperatures of thousands of degrees. The heat of the earth could feed on two sources of energy: in the beginning, on the kinetic energy of the fragments that combined to form the earth; since then, and until today, on the nuclear energy of the radio-active elements contained in the rock.

If we watch a meteorite being slowed down by the earth's atmosphere, we can observe even today how the kinetic energy of a fragment falling upon the earth with cosmic speed is converted into heat. An ordinary shooting star, plainly visible to the naked eye, lights up at a height of sixty miles, yet it weighs only a small fraction of an ounce. It is conceivable that this source of energy alone was sufficient to maintain the earth in a hot-liquid state during the period of its formation. It is certain that throughout the two or three billion years of its existence, and up to the present day, the earth has received a uniform internal supply of energy from radio-activity. A considerable amount of energy is freed in the decay of every radio-active atomic nucleus. We know what amounts of radio-active matter are contained in the rocks that form the crust of the earth, and we have calculated that even in a fairly thin surface layer of the earth as much energy is produced by radio-activity as the earth radiates away into space. In fact, we find it hard to understand why with this supply of energy the temperature of the earth is not constantly increasing.

The structure of the earth tells us that at some time in the past the earth must have been sufficiently liquid to allow the free flow of matter. Measurements have established that the innermost portions of the earth have a higher specific weight than the crust. It is very likely that the core of the earth consists of iron and nickel. There are differences in the chemical composition of the crust also. The great continents are of a lighter substance than the floor of the ocean. Like ice floes, the continents float on the heavier matter underneath. None of these separations of substance could have occurred if the body of the earth had been completely rigid. Again, it is not necessary to assume that the interior of the earth has ever been, even less still is, as liquid as water. With the high pressures prevailing in the lower strata of the earth, the difference between a liquid and a solid is much smaller than the differences we observe in our daily surroundings. High pres-

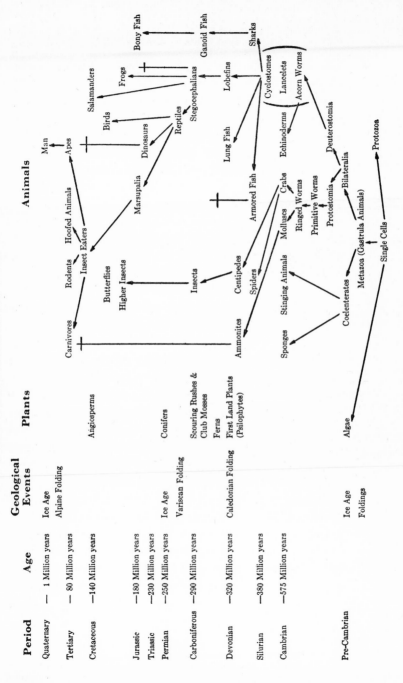

GEOLOGICAL-PALAEONTOLOGICAL TABLE

sure can make a thin liquid viscous, and can cause solid matter to flow slowly.

If the earth ever has been hotter and more fluid than it is today, it must have cooled off rapidly. There is no reason to assume that it cooled off gradually over the last two billion years. On the contrary, as I said earlier, we are hard put to avoid the opposite conclusion, a conclusion that also could not be reconciled with geological experience. Physically, the earth has achieved balance long ago. Volcanoes and the formation of mountains show that this balance is still subject to occasional though only superficial disturbances.

Mountains and volcanoes lead us to consider the historic ages of the earth that form the special study of geology. As we did with the stars, we shall begin with a survey of the phenomena before venturing an explanation.

I have tabulated the most important dates in the history of the earth. We shall go over the columns of this table from left to right.

In the first column are shown the names of the geological periods. Next come the ages of the periods, that is, the time that elapsed from the beginning of the period to the present, expressed in millions of years. I have used the most recent figures available to me. The extent to which these figures may still be inaccurate might be indicated by the following example: The age of the Tertiary could very well be sixty instead of eighty million years, but it could certainly not be as little as forty. The age of the Cambrian might conceivably be five hundred, or even seven hundred, but it could hardly be four hundred or eight hundred million years.

Next follow two important classes of events in the physical history of the earth, the building of mountains, and the ice ages. Great mountain systems come about by a folding of the crust of the earth—their articulation into distinct chains of folds is clearly shown in the structure of young ranges such as the Alps. Mountains are not enduring formations. Ice, water, and wind level them off, and a mountain system may be flattened out fifty million years after it has arisen. However, in the folding process the masses have been pressed not only upward but also, and even to a larger extent, downward. The visible mountain, like the visible portion of an iceberg, is only a small part of the entire mass. Thus there is left in the crust of the earth a solid block of the old formation, and if the crust moves once more later on, the upper part of this block may rise again as a minor mountain chain. The mountains of central Germany are an example of a block that underwent such a secondary rising. They originated in the Variscan mountain-buildings of the Carboniferous period. The Norwegian and Scottish mountain systems rose in the earlier Caledonian disturbance. Other portions of the earth, not now rising as mountains, such as the Norwegian-Finnish regions, are still older mountainous ground. We must not forget that the known geological periods cover only a fourth or a fifth of the life of the earth.

The history of the earth is thus a continuous sequence of mountain-buildings and erosions. Smaller foldings must be inserted between the high points shown in our table. The great periods, however, still stand out clearly. We are now living close to one of the great mountain-building periods—we are almost still within that period: the Alps are still rising even today. Only rarely in the history of the earth have the mountains been as high as they are just now. High mountains usually go together with large continents and deep oceans. When the mountains have been leveled down, the continents are smaller and lower, the oceans larger but shallower. Of the two phases that constitute this cycle of the mountains, the leveling-off is immediately evident to us. With our own eyes we see how rocks roll from the mountains down into the valley, and how the rivers carry away gravel and sand. But what force is it that builds the mountains up again and again?

This force cannot come from the folded continental masses themselves, but must stem from the foundation on which the continents are floating. In the past it was thought that the earth is shrinking as it cools off, and that the crust of the earth is wrinkling up in the process like the skin of a drying apple. This theory is false. Even its first assumption is incorrect—the earth has not grown noticeably cooler for billions of years. Even so, it remains probably true that the building of mountains is connected with the heat supply in the center of the earth. The opinion most generally held today is that, rather than a cooling-off, a temporary overheating due to radio-activity produces the movements of the lower strata which show up as folding activities on the surface of the earth. For instance, overheated fragments in the core of the earth might be rising while others are sinking, and the resulting currents in the foundations of the earth, circling slowly through millions of years, might carry along, compress, and fold the masses resting upon them. Wegener has advanced the well-known hypothesis that the continents of America and Europe-Africa have hung together at one time, and have been slowly moving away from each other for several hundred million years, while the sea, the Atlantic Ocean, is filling the growing rift. Wegener's theory is still in dispute today. But if it is true, this migration of continents, too, is most likely connected with currents inside the earth.

An ice age follows some of the greatest mountain-building periods. This sequence alone makes it seem likely that the ice ages have geological rather than cosmic causes. Variations in the radiation of the sun, that have been called upon in an attempt to determine the chronology of the most recent glacial period, the Quaternary, can at best modify the course of the ice age. The variations cannot be the decisive cause of the ice ages for the simple reason that they must have been about the same throughout the history of the earth, while the ice ages have been very rare. The true cause of the ice ages is still unknown. Perhaps they are due to changes in climate brought about by the rising of mountain systems, and by the consequent great extension of continents. If this is the case, it would support what I have said in the second chapter, namely that we are living in a mild interval in the midst of an ice age, and that new glaciations covering our country might be expected perhaps ten thousand years from now.

We are now turning to the history of life on earth. I shall give here merely a survey of the facts. Details and an interpretation of the facts will be the subject of the remaining chapters.

A well-documented history of life can be written from

the Cambrian period on. This does not mean that life did not begin before the Cambrian. We possess older traces of life, and above all we have a convincing theory why earlier life has left us so few documents. Until deep into the Silurian, life existed only in the sea. Hence, we can find traces of the life of earlier times only in those regions that were then covered by the sea, and that are dry land today: for where there is sea today we cannot dig. Now a portion of the earth's surface has always been sea, for instance, the Pacific Ocean; another portion has always been dry land, for instance, the Canadian, Central Asiatic, and Finnish-Swedish massifs. This leaves only those formerly low portions of the continents that were covered by water during the periods when the oceans were greatly extended. Now, for a long time previous to the Cambrian period, the continents were very large. What is land today was for the most part land then also. During that time, life may have developed a great wealth of forms. The Cambrian opened with an advance of the sea over portions of land that today are dry once more. The sea brought life with it, and this is why the wealth of fossils begins for us with the Cambrian deposits.

For the pre-Cambrian ages, we must rely entirely on indirect conclusions. The most important question is: How did life come to be? Up until today we have no answer. But I fail to see how we can avoid assuming an original generation, that is, the growth of molecules or groups of molecules of the kind we call alive, out of those that we do not yet call alive. I shall reserve for the next chapter the fundamental question whether the origin and growth of life can be described at all within the conceptual framework of present-day scientific thinking. Reaching ahead of my subject, I shall present here merely a train of thought that bears on our problem and that, to me at least, carries conviction.

All living beings that we know have parents. This corresponds to the statement I formulated in the sixth chapter, that forms can come only out of such other forms that are similar to them in their degree of differentiation. Since the earth itself has only a finite age, this series of forebears must have had a beginning. According to the law just mentioned of the continuity in the origin of forms, the forms at the beginning of the series must then have been of a kind that could originate with physico-chemical probability on a planet which itself had just come into existence. In other words, simple molecules must probably have been the beginning of the series of forebears. There is to my knowledge only one other physically tenable theory that seems to escape this necessity, and that is the assumption that germs of life have reached the earth out of the universe from other already inhabited stars. But if the whole universe is only slightly older than the earth, then this assumption, too, does not advance us very much.

The history of the simplest living things remains unknown to us. It is difficult to decide whether our present virus molecules are similar to those simplest beings, or whether they are not rather a later parasitic, "degenerate" form of life. At one time or another life must have reached the form of organization that we call a cell. From that stage onward, we gain some few indications from the order of beings living today. Beings that are related in their form may also be related in their ancestry. The separation into the two great branches, plants and animals, begins even in single-celled beings. If for a moment we disregard secondary acquired qualities, we can express the difference between plants and animals thus: Plants feed on inanimate matter, animals on animate matter, that is, on plants or other animals. Plants, therefore, could exist without animals, but animals could not exist without plants. Nature generally takes advantage of the possibilities that are open to her, hence we may perhaps say more pointedly: Animals need not exist in order that plants may exist. But if there are plants, animals can and therefore do exist. For every being, after a while, will meet another one that feeds on it.

I shall barely touch upon the evolution of plants. The oldest plants of which we have traces are the one-celled sea-algae. From our point of view, the most important advance the plants have made has been the conquest of dry land, beginning with the late Silurian. Up until then the continents, whether dry or humid, had been lifeless deserts. The first plants that climbed onto the land kept their roots still in the shallow waters of the shore. Gradually they advanced farther. At first, they were leafless and long-stemmed. In the Devonian period, a great variety of forms developed. The forests of the Carboniferous period, out of which our mineral coal has come, consisted of scouring rushes and club moss trees. The flowering plants covering the earth today are of very recent origin. The scent of flowers, the humming of bees, and the twittering of birds have been known only for about one hundred million years.

I shall discuss at somewhat greater length the evolution

of animals. Their pre-Cambrian beginnings can be disclosed only by drawing conclusions from the existing order of zoölogy. Single-celled beings or protozoa must have existed from the beginnings until today. Some of them have built up whole mountains out of their siliciferous or calciferous shells and skeletons. Yet up to this day new forms are developing among them. The viruses, for example, that cause the specific diseases of the higher animals and of man, could acquire their special adaptation only after the higher animals had come into existence.

Evolutionary progress was achieved by the many-celled beings or metazoa. Several cells that have come from a single cell remain together, and divide among themselves the functions necessary for the maintenance of life. Just as the social division of labor among men is the basis of culture, so the division of labor among the cells is the basis of a more differentiated form of life. The simplest metazoa may have combined into a sack with an opening, enclosing a cavity. This structure is still found in a certain stage of the embryonic development of all higher animals, and is called the *gastrula*. The coelenterates, animals with a hollow, spherical body, have retained this structure once and for all. The main species of coelenterates were represented already during the Cambrian. Even in those days there were sponges, and the two forms of stinging fish—the free-floating jellyfish, and sedentary polyps.

The animals of the other main branch, called bilateralia because of their two-sided symmetry, have a second opening in their bodies, beside the original one which is called "original mouth." This structure creates a body channel, mouth-food pipe-stomach-intestines-anus, such as we still have in our own bodies. Animals of this type again fall into two groups, the protostomia in whom the original mouth developed into the mouth, and the deuterostomia whose mouth developed from the secondary opening. In either group, the other opening developed into the anus. Protostomia and deuterostomia, too, had already separated in pre-Cambrian times, and have since developed along different lines. At the end of the evolution of the protostomia there is the state-forming instinct of termites, bees, and ants. At the end of the evolution of the deuterostomia there is the state-forming intelligence of man.

The evolution of the protostomia leads over primitive worms to ringed worms with segmented bodies, such as our earthworm. Ringed worms are found as early as the Cambrian period, as are their descendants the molluscs, for instance, clams, snails, squids, and also crabs. Geologically the most famous molluscs are the ammonites whose spiral shells are among the most frequently found fossils particularly in Jurassic and Triassic formations. With the exception of a few primitive relics, this branch of animals died out during the Cretaceous period. Spiders stem either from early crabs or directly from the ringed worms; centipedes without a doubt stem from crabs. From the centipedes, insects developed during the Carboniferous period. Since the dry land now offers vegetation for food, it is accessible also to the animals, and the animals soon conquer the air as well. Among the first insects are dragon-flies with a wing span of up to thirty inches. Butterflies, and the so-called orthoptera, among which belong bees and ants, have existed only since the Jurassic period. It is obvious that the great expansion of flowering plants went hand in hand with that of the insects pollinating them.

The most primitive deuterostomia we know are likewise worm-shaped—the acorn worms. The evolution leading from them to the lancelet fish and to the cyclostomes (among them the river lamprey) is known to us only by inference from the systematic order of zoölogy. A side-branch are the prickly-skinned echinoderms such as star fish, sea urchin, sea-gherkin, and other marine growth. In the Silurian the first fishes appear—the structure of the vertebrates acquires its present form. By and large it may be said that protostomia support their body by shells, vertebrates by a skeleton. The fishes soon develop a wealth of forms. Two of these have become of great consequence. The sharks have become the ancestors of almost all fish known to us. The lobe-finned crossopterygii have led up to the land vertebrates. Just as the lung-fish of to-day, they possessed a swim bladder adapted to breathing air, and crawled about in the original mud at the water's edge. We can follow their development through several intermediate stages to the stegocephalians or "roof-headed" amphibians. The stegocephalians had converted their fins into short legs and become amphibians. From them, the development leads to frogs and salamanders as well as to reptiles.

The first reptiles were adapted to a life led entirely on dry land. They produced the most formidable family of animals prior to the mammals to hold dominion over the earth: the great dinosaurs that spread over the dry land, over the sea, and through the air. A relic of the dinosaurs are today's crocodiles, and the mythical image of the dragon (I do not know the origin of this image) may give us an impression of how terrible they have been. Snakes, lizards, turtles belong to the reptiles. The birds are descended from them. The development of some early forms of reptiles of the Southern Hemisphere finally leads to the mammals.

The most important achievement of the birds and the mammals is their constant body temperature. It allows them to carry on, with uniformly high vitality, under changing conditions in the environment. It has opened to them the night and the Arctic zone, and has made them superior to their competitors even under normal conditions.

Originally, the mammals may have been similar to our present egg-laying duckbills. Later on, they lived through long ages in the form of marsupalia, pouched animals, of which Australia has preserved a relic to the present day. The first mammals of a more familiar structure appear toward the end of the Cretaceous period. They are insect eaters related to our shrew-mouse. It is of course no accident that this line began after flowering plants and insects had come into existence.

The main families of mammals are present in the early Tertiary. In some cases we can follow their development in detail throughout the Tertiary. The best-known case is the horse. The first horses, such as have been found for instance in the Geisel valley, were so small that modern man could easily hold them in the palm of his hand. We know all the intervening stages up to the present horse.

The development of the apes begins with half-apes or prosimians, closely related to the insect eaters. The development continues up to the division between the apes of the Old World and those of the New, and in the Old World up to the anthropoids notable for their intelligence.

From the anthropoids, the line points toward man. The significance of this last step is the subject of the final chapter.

IX
Life

W E HAVE surveyed the outer history of life. In
doing so we have used the term "life" naïvely. But,
finally, what is this all-familiar and mysterious thing that
we call life? And what are the forces that have determined
its origin?

We look on life these days from two opposing points of
view, from man, and from physical science. My horse, my
dog, they are my playmates in the game of life, and closer
to me than many a human being. An amoeba, an alga, a
fungus on the other hand, mean hardly more to me than
quaint physical objects with properties that I find it difficult to explain. Nor is it possible to draw a dividing line
somewhere through life and to declare that below this
line physical science applies, above it human understanding. We may be able to formulate precise concepts with
the help of borderline cases. But the transitions in the
understanding of reality which we gain by these concepts
are no less fluid than are the transitions within historical
evolution itself. Let us recall how in the second chapter
we gradually reduced the understanding that exists between man and man, until we had arrived at the mathematical laws of nature, and, conversely, how in the three

preceding chapters the series of forms from the primeval mist up to man unfolded before us. Even when there were gaps in our knowledge, at no time was there a compelling necessity to assume discontinuity of evolution. The cleavage between subject and object is not in nature, it is in our thinking—or, it is in nature only insofar as she has produced us and our thinking. There are not two different kinds of things in nature. It is only we who see things in two different ways.

These remarks are so far a confession of belief rather than a scientific insight. To what extent can they be converted into an insight? We do not have today a basis of assured knowledge, raised and removed above the conflict. For the time being, then, we can do nothing else than study, and compare carefully, what we observe from both opposing points of view. Perhaps in this way the right order of relation will at some time reveal itself to us. We must follow the circle of the twofold coherence between subject and object, and must not be afraid to follow the direction that is proper to either half-circle, into all its consequences, even though seemingly it is opposed to that of the other half-circle. It is the extremes that touch each other fruitfully, not hasty compromises. The more completely we follow the sweep of our circle, the larger the area we will encompass. Only if we break away from the round, only if we forget the turn of the other half that is always waiting for us, only then do we tear asunder what belongs together.

For the realm of organic life, the peculiar coherence of the two half-circles is expressed in the two statements I made in the second chapter: *Being is older than knowl-*

edge, but *only knowledge knows what being is.* We see perfection in the hand of an ape, and in the organization of a beehive, but ape and bee do not. They are perfect but do not know it. That is why they constantly invite us to study them from the two opposing points of view. They are intelligible, and so we understand them from the point of view of man's intelligence. They are unconscious, and so we understand them from the point of view of unconscious nature, that is, in physical terms. I intend in this chapter to carry the interpretation in physical terms as far as possible. The result will show how much of what is commonly expressed in human terms, can be derived from physical interpretation. To prove this point is the most important task here before me. For it is my belief that this and only this proof constitutes a solid foundation for a bridge between subject and object that might be built in the future.

Biology, in the last few decades, has given expression to the dualistic approach in the fundamental conflict between mechanists and vitalists. Let me first describe both positions.

A living organism, understood in physical terms, is a certain kind of material system. The organism, though engaged in a constant interchange of substance with its surroundings, can be distinguished from them with a certain degree of accuracy. Living organisms consist of some of the same chemical elements that make up their inorganic surroundings. We have succeeded, in the laboratory, in producing a large measure of the specific "organic" combinations of elements that occur in living things. This suggests the idea that, given sufficient knowledge of the internal structure of organisms, we should be able to explain the origin and behavior of organisms entirely in physical and chemical terms. This hypothesis is known as the thesis of mechanism. The name is unfortunate since neither physics nor chemistry is any longer based on mechanics. We would perhaps do better to call it physicism.

It is not quite as simple to reduce to a formula the counter-thesis which usually has called itself vitalism. All of the vitalistic trends share the negative conviction that physics and chemistry alone are not enough to explain life. Their various positive convictions, however, emerge only when we press for an answer to the specific question just what it is in life that escapes physical science.

I shall accept immediately as true a positive formulation which, however, is not yet typically vitalistic: Physics cannot be expected to give answers to questions that cannot be asked in terms of physics. The physicist, with the means at his command, does not perceive the subjective side of life, soul, sentiment, consciousness. Therefore he cannot hope to explain that side of life in his terms. No conceptual system can produce results containing concepts that are not defined within the system. The decisive methodological self-limitation of the physicist consists in that he does not even ask, what is the soul. And as long as physics abides by this limitation, obviously it cannot give information about the soul. I myself intend to accept the limitation for the present chapter.

But I also want to insist on the reverse of what I have just said: If a question can be asked in terms of physics, and if it has any answer at all, we must expect that the answer can be found with the means of physics. All questions that relate to the physical structure and behavior of organisms, now, are clearly concerned with material processes. Hence, they are questions that can be asked in terms of physics. And insofar as they have any answers at all, I believe these answers can be given without going beyond the frame of reference of physical science.

These remarks are already contradicting vitalism even before I have given a positive formulation of its thesis. Vitalism can in fact be defined as the particular tendency to discover processes which can be demonstrated physically but which, supposedly, cannot be explained in physical terms. This tendency usually goes hand in hand with efforts to make the specific characteristics of such physically unexplained processes the starting point for a non-physical explanation of life. I believe a discussion of these efforts will be instructive for our further inquiry. Some of them are based on general notions concerning the nature of life and of physical science, some on specific facts of experience. Both deserve critical study.

What is the fundamental motive of the vitalist? Mechanism strikes him as shallow. He feels that the study of physical processes leaves out the essence of life. This essence is what he wants to emphasize. Let me assume that so far the vitalist is right. But what follows? Either, that the essence of life remains altogether invisible on the physical level. If so, we ought to leave off all physical inquiry and look for the essence where it is. Or, that a closer look would show the essence in the physical processes themselves. If so, we ought to practice looking closely. But in this second case it does not seem consistent to me that gaps in the coherence of the physical world should even be thought desirable.

May I use an example from the history of physics to illustrate this to me most important point? The natural scientists of early modern times, growing out of the world of Christendom, comprehended under the name of God all that which is ultimately essential for man. Therefore, the relation of science to God was a crucial question for them. When Copernicus and Kepler studied the geometrical structure of the planetary system, they did not believe that the essence would escape them. On the contrary, they thought it was precisely in the validity of the mathematical laws that they would seize upon the spirit in nature, upon the creative idea of God. When Newton later on explained Kepler's laws in terms of mechanics, it was held that the workings of the planetary system had now been explained in profane terms, so to speak, and the peculiar question arose whether this view of the world left any room for God. The one remaining indication of what now was termed the direct intercession of an intelligent creator was seen in the fact that at that time the origin and the stability of the planetary system still defied mechanical explanation. The gap in knowledge became the argument for the existence of God. This is probably the worst possible form of proof of the existence of God. For gaps in knowledge have a habit of closing—and God is no stopgap. Laplace proved the stability of the planetary system, rendered its mechanical origin probable, and declined to speak of God. It seems to me that there are three possible attitudes, each clear within itself, which might be named after these three men: Kepler, Pascal,

Laplace. Kepler could experience God in the mathematical law of nature. Pascal could not. But since his concern was God, he sacrificed the study of mathematics to what was more important, and sought God where He could be found. Laplace neither could nor would find God in mathematics, and so he spoke of what is mathematically demonstrable, and left God alone.

Later modern times have often used the concept of life in a semi-religious sense. One spoke of life where he did not dare speak of God. A concept of life for which a place has to be made by interrupting the physical coherences, seems to me a stopgap twice over. This concept substitutes itself for a god who, in turn, can be recognized only by the gaps in those laws that he himself created. I myself would say that we do not fail in true reverence for life if we acknowledge complete physical coherence in the material processes of life. True, for us who are alive ourselves, living beings cannot be objects merely of physical knowledge. But what we owe them beyond that, what we owe them above all, is not the denial of the substance of objective knowledge, it is that which joins the "I" to the "Thou"—love. If knowledge excludes us from love, we must give up knowledge. But even then the substance of knowledge does not cease being true in the sense in which physical science claims it to be true.

Before discussing the empirical grounds of vitalism, I must define exactly in what sense I intend to use the concept of physical knowledge. Both physics and chemistry are themselves in a process of evolution. It seems imprudent to assume that precisely the state of knowledge which the two sciences have reached today must be sufficient to understand the biological facts. We can define physics in very general terms as the empirical, rational, objectifying method of the exact sciences for the gathering of facts. This definition alone would exclude most forms of vitalism. But what I said earlier, that if a question can be asked in terms of physics, and if it has any answer at all, we must expect that the answer can be found with the means of physics—this statement has wider implications. It presupposes not only that physics is a method of thinking, but also that it possesses a conceptual system. Furthermore, the statement is not self-evident even in pure physics. The advance from classical physics to the theory of relativity and the quantum theory was due specifically to the fact that questions were being raised in classical physics that could no longer be answered in classical physics. We are hoping today to advance in the same fashion, through the unsolved problems of the quantum theory, to an as yet unknown theory of the elementary particles. There is a widespread conviction today even among physicists that physics will have to be expanded in a similar manner if we are to arrive at an understanding of life; it is assumed that there are specific laws of life, and that the laws of inanimate matter are borderline cases of the laws of life, just as classical physics is a borderline case of the quantum theory. I myself would doubt the necessity for such an expansion of physics unless what is intended is the introduction into physics of the subject. The phenomena of life, much unlike those of the atomic nucleus, lie well within the spatial dimensions in which the laws of physics as we know them have proved their validity. Viewed in terms of matter, life takes place either in the atomic shell or in larger complexes of atoms. The phenomena of life will no doubt force us yet to raise new questions, but they may not force us to introduce new basic laws. The only thing that seems imperative to me is that we take proper heed of the historic character of physical events. This is the point at which we must turn to the specific problems experience presents to us. Where is it that the phenomena of life make physical interpretation difficult?

The oldest non-physical scientific notion of life operates with the idea of purpose. We call this notion teleological or final. It does not ask: "How did man get his hand?" but: "What does man have his hand for?" The answer is obvious enough, man has his hand for grasping things. In the same way, the bird has wings for flying, all animals have mouths for eating and sex organs for propagation. The original meaning of the word "organ" is "working tool." The teleological form of inquiry is so obviously reasonable that it simply cannot be avoided, not even in present-day biology. The inquiry into the purpose of an organ is not yet a part of theory, it is a part of the inventory of facts. We do not know the organ until we know its function.

I have just substituted the word function for the word purpose. This adaptation to current usage may serve us to clarify the problems involved in the concept of purpose. If used as the ultimate principle of explanation, purpose encounters at least three fundamental difficulties. First, there are phenomena in organism that we must consider not only as purposeless, but as running counter to all purpose. What part does the vermiform appendix play in our life except that of occasionally infecting? Secondly, the question for the purpose does not render superfluous the question for the cause. Even if I know that I can use my hand to take hold of things, I am still far from knowing how it happens that I have a hand. Finalism made into the sole principle is like the faith in a good fairy who grants immediate fulfilment for every wish. And thirdly, the concept of purpose is derived from man's consciousness. There is purpose in nature, but we cannot distinguish a consciousness bent on accomplishing the purpose. The statement that being is older than knowledge is particularly true of the idea of purpose.

Because of these difficulties, vitalism has usually substituted other concepts for that of purpose. These other concepts often furnish a convincing description of the phenomena of life. But the question remains open whether or not the phenomena are necessarily and fundamentally incapable of physical explanation. What distinguishes the living organism is that it retains a constant form while changing its substance, that it has an individuality, and the faculties of procreation, regeneration, and self-stabilization. But cannot physical objects have these faculties just as well? We say, "a machine cannot repair itself." This saying illustrates only that a machine is a very poor physical simile for life. Let us take instead so simple a thing as the flame of a candle. No one will deny that the flame can be understood in physico-chemical terms. And yet, it changes its substance while retaining its form, it regenerates its form after outside disturbances, it can multiply (if we light other candles with it), and last but not least, it lends itself to the very same experiment that

Driesch performed on sea-urchins: if we split the wick, two complete though weaker candle flames come into existence. The reader may think this is sophistry. I do not believe so. It is not for nothing that fire has been the symbol of life since earliest times. Could two phenomena that are so similar be essentially so different?

But enough of criticism. How shall the physicist understand life? The theory of evolution is the decisive step in the direction of such understanding. Life is a historic phenomenon. There is no doubt that living things are by far the most differentiated forms on earth. If differentiation can advance only gradually, then the most differentiated forms must have the longest history. And this is exactly what we learn also from geological experience. It has been said that if life could be understood in physical terms, then we ought to be able to produce living things. One of the possible replies would be: What has come to be through history, can be reproduced only by a repetition of its history. Living things can come to be if the necessary conditions are present. The conditions are: the crust of the earth and two billion years' time.

However, we are not satisfied with the mere fact of evolution. We are concerned with its causes. What are the forces that could bring about all these amazing forms? An answer to this question which is merely hypothetical and yet, I think, by far the most remarkable answer ever given, is Darwin's theory of natural selection. Darwinism has its opponents even today. But it is my opinion that no one has the right to criticize the superficialities perpetrated by many Darwinists when they passed judgment in matters of the mind, until he has fully understood the

tremendous power of clarification this theory possesses
if it is taken purely as a hypothesis of natural science.
The remainder of this chapter will convey, I hope, some
of this clarifying power.

Darwin declares that organisms have developed
through natural selection in the fight for life. This assertion contains two theses that can conceptually be separated. The first is almost self-evident. Let me express it
this way: What is fit to live remains alive. This is little
more than a definition of "fit to live." But it is also evidence that the causal and the final aspects can be studied
together. No wonder the forms alive today are fit to live—
if they weren't, they would have perished long ago. The
ultimate purpose of every organ, as far as we can determine, seems to be always the preservation either of the
individual or of the species. If a large number of species
join in the fight for life at any one time, certainly those
among them will in the end survive that are fittest in this
sense. In this way fitness becomes an objective concept.
The purposes of nature are real, even though there is no
consciousnss that conceives them.

So far, the theory of natural selection is unassailable.
But what is fit can survive only after it has come into
existence. How did it come into existence? At this point
Darwin's second and somewhat more doubtful thesis
takes over: What is fit has come into existence by chance.
Let me express this immediately in modern terms: The
chromosomes of the cell center carry the units of heredity
or genes. The genes undergo occasional changes or mutations. The mutations that have been observed occur according to chance. We cannot discern in them any pref-

erence for what would serve a purpose. For instance, light-eyed animals may have red-eyed offspring, or long-legged animals short-legged offspring. Most mutations of this sort reduce the animal's fitness for life. This fact is readily understood, because the qualities of any living being usually constitute a well balanced whole, and any change in detail almost invariably means a loss. But now and then mutations may occur that will immediately make the individual more fit for life. Again, a faculty may arise that becomes advantageous only under changed conditions, or only in combination with other newly arising faculties. To a fish living exclusively in the water, it means no advantage that its swim bladder develops into an organ for breathing air. But if such a fish lives near the shore, the change enables it to crawl onto dry land, and to become the ancestor of the land vertebrates.

Darwinists today are convinced that chance and selection have been sufficient to bring about the evolution of organisms. This thesis is under dispute among scientists. As a non-specialist I cannot join in the dispute. But I am free, I believe, to voice the impression I gain as an onlooker. Most of the specific objections to Darwinism can be formulated this way: "I cannot imagine how this or that phenomenon, say, the eye of the vertebrate or the state organization of the ants, could have come about merely by chance and selection." However, *I cannot imagine* is a poor argument in science. Newton could not imagine how the all-embracing, unifying order of the planetary system could have come about mechanically. Kant and Laplace have imagined it, and chances are they imagined it rather correctly. With the great multiplicity of historic forms, we cannot insist on a precise explanation of a specific detail. It is enough if we can see the possible origin of an increasing number of details. And it may well be said that the study of evolution allows us to do just that.

But I wish to analyze somewhat more closely the conceptual structure of the theory of natural selection. I should like to raise the question what view of nature we accept when we subscribe to this theory.

The theory of natural selection presupposes the historic character of time. First of all, the theory endows time with a direction, since it teaches an evolution in which the less differentiated forms are in the past, the more differentiated ones in the future. Next, the theory employs the historic character of time as the driving force of that evolution. That is implied in its most obscure concept, chance. What is chance? We call a chance event one whose necessity we do not see, an event that was merely possible until it had become a fact. Hence we must note two things in a chance event—that it was possible in the first place, and that it becomes a fact.

In order to come into existence at all, every organic form must be physically possible. Darwinism presupposes that possibility. Here Darwinism reveals its limitations, but also its harmlessness. That the world is made in such a way that a howling monkey can actually exist, and that this form composed of atoms constitutes a whole which is able to function—for this no proof is offered. Only experience proves it: what is real must be possible. All that is positively asserted is that the body of the howling monkey, whose existence is known from experience, satisfies the laws of physics. If this assertion is true, then the monkey has existed potentially since the beginning of the world, because the laws of physics which have been in force since then permitted its existence. The forms that have arisen show how immeasurably rich in possibilities nature has always been. And the marvel of an actual form is hardly less than the marvel of a simple law containing in itself the possibility of this form, and of countless other forms besides. The theory of natural selection merely claims to show a way in which these possible forms could become real. The forms that have become real on earth are presumably not the only forms possible. It may be that on other, similar stars life has been led by chance along entirely different paths.

It has been held that chance could create only disorder, and hence was in harmony with the Second Law, but that for this very reason it could not be reconciled with the evolution of forms. I have shown in the sixth chapter that both the Second Law and the evolution of forms follow equally from the historic character of time. The source of energy that feeds the growth of forms on earth is the sun. The earth, no less than the universe, was void and empty in the beginning. Soon there is such an abundance of the simplest forms that generation and destruction hold each other the balance. Evolution is the process by which more and more differentiated forms emerge in time from the ocean of mere possibilities. The forms are related by birth. Not everything that could exist can come to be, its line of ancestors likewise must consist entirely of possible forms. Not everything that can come to be survives. Objective fitness in the fight for life makes the selection.

It has been asked whether what we call chance events are events whose determining causes are unknown, or events that simply do not have a cause. This question is irrelevant to our present reflections. The historic character of time does not depend on our ability to reduce the possibility of future events to a complete or partial necessity. Much can be said for the assumption that mutations are essentially unpredictable in terms of physics. It seems that mutations are due to elementary chemical action such as the transposition of a single atom within a molecule. And according to quantum theory, such elementary action can absolutely not be predicted except with probability.

Some closing remarks should be devoted to the concepts "individual" and "death." What is an individual? Physically, it is first of all a mass of matter, distinguishable from its surroundings, continuous, and of a specific form. Stars, molecules, or crystals are also individuals in this sense. Living individuals have in addition a temporal form. They are brought forth by their own likes, bring forth others like themselves, and die. Propagation and death belong to the individual life. For the "virtually immortal" single-celled things, procreation and death are one and the same act, the cell division; the individual ceases to exist because it splits up into two of the same kind. In the higher animals, the two acts are separate but presuppose each other. The individual has to procreate only because death is part of its scheme of life—else the species would die out. The individual has to die only because procreation is part of its scheme of life—for more than a certain number of individuals of the same species cannot exist at one time. The concept of the species, as the totality of individuals of the same heredity and whose preservation is served by purposeful organs, is a meaningful concept only because there is death and procreation.

Why are organisms not immortal? Molecules and crystals are in a sense immortal. They may perish, to be sure, but only through destruction by an outside agent. It is generally thought that organisms wear out in the course of their life, and that this is why they have to die. But why do they have to wear out? Germ plasm does not wear out. Life is as fresh today as it was five hundred million years ago. Only the individuals change. If immortality had offered an advantage in the struggle for existence, should life not have been capable of creating immortal organisms?

I believe, rather, that the mortality of organisms is objectively purposeful in the sense in which the theory of natural selection allows us to use the term. We must distinguish three degrees of purpose: purpose for the individual, purpose for the species, and purpose for the generation of new forms. Eyes, mouth, and stomach serve the preservation of the individual. Sex organs and breeding instinct profit the individual itself nothing (except possibly by their secondary effects), but they serve the preservation of the species. Finally, there may also be properties that do not serve any purpose of preservation but are useful for the generation of new forms. If two species that are otherwise equally fit oppose each other in the fight for life, the offspring of that species will win out which is quicker to develop new and more perfect variants. Therefore, properties that enrich or quicken evolution will maintain themselves. The diploidy of the chromosomes, which is the factor that introduces fertilization into the process of procreation, and hence is the factor responsible for sexuality, is believed to have this quality of quickening and enriching evolution. Mortality too, I believe, quickens evolution.

Evolution can be the faster, the more individuals of a species are living in a given period of time, because the number of mutations that are being tested then is larger in proportion. The number of individuals that can live at any one time is limited by space and quantity of food available. Therefore, the number of individuals within a given time span is larger in proportion as the generations follow one another more rapidly. In Darwinian terms, there is bound to be selective pressure in favor of short-lived individuals. On the other hand, a differentiated physical structure requires for its growth a certain minimum length of time. The polarity of these two factors probably determines the actual life span of the individual.

Only mortality and procreation produce the surplus of individuals and with it the fight for life that is the driving force of evolution. Life develops onward because each living thing is on the brink of death. Such is the paradoxical situation of the individual: It kills in order to live, and lives in order to die. It has offspring that can live only if the individual itself dies, and that is destined to die in the same way. The individual would never have come to be if it did not share with all its ancestors this disposition, that it wants to live, and that it has to die. And this, now, is no mere objective process involving remote physical forms. It is our own destiny, and we experience it subjectively, because the individual is also the repository of the feeling and conscious soul.

X

The Soul

WE CAN no longer leave the soul out of our reflections. What is the soul? What is its relation to the body? What do we know of its history?

Only with reference to his own self does man have an equally immediate knowledge of both body and soul. Thus we must first learn to see the reality of the soul in man before we can trace its history in the animal kingdom. We know the soul as the "I," as the "thou," and as the "we." Our philosophical tradition makes it simplest to talk of the "I." This is the only reason why in this chapter I shall discuss the soul as the "I."

We begin with physics, in order to define our frontiers with the realm of physics. The human body is made up of the same chemical elements as the inorganic world, obeys the same laws, and presumably has developed out of inorganic stuff in a manner that can be understood in terms of physics. The temptation to say "Now we know what man is. Man is nothing but matter," is very strong. Such a statement represents what we would call naïve materialism. What are the objections to this position? It might be criticized on two counts: that it gives the false appearance of an explanation, and the words "nothing but."

Materialism believes to have achieved an understanding of man when he has been reduced to matter. To dispel this illusion we need only ask: "And what is matter?" In atomic physics, matter is defined by its possible reactions to human experiments, and by the mathematical—that is, intellectual—laws it obeys. We are defining matter as a possible object of man's manipulation. Thus the statement that "man is matter" merely draws us into the circle of which I have spoken so often. The statement is capable of an interpretation in which it is correct, but it does not by itself explain to us man's essence. It is an invitation that we round the circle where man and matter presuppose and depend on one another.

And then, the statement does not tell everything we know of man. It does not tell what is to us the most important. Here are a few examples:

Light of 6000 Å wave length reaches my eye. From the retina, a chemico-electrical stimulus passes through the optical nerve into the brain where it sets off another stimulus of certain motor nerves, and out of my mouth come the words: "The apple is red." Nowhere in this description of the process, complete though it is, has any mention been made that I have had the color perception "red." Of sense perception, nothing was said.

I pluck the apple and give it to my child. The child laughs and eats it. I stand and watch. Nowhere in this description has any mention been made of the child's delight, or of my delight at his delight. Of the experience of the soul, nothing was said.

I hear the sound: "The apple is red." There is no mention anywhere in this statement that it is a phrase intended to express a set of facts, and that the facts are true. Of the act of judgment which can comprehend a set of facts in accordance with the truth, nothing was said.

Sense perception, experience of the soul, and judgment —they belong to the subjective side of man. What is their relation to man's material side?

There is the old doctrine that man is made up of two substances, body and soul. This dualism avoids the mistake made by naïve materialism of forgetting the soul. But in turn it sacrifices an insight materialism possessed, even though materialism did not express it rightly: namely, that body and soul are after all the same man. "I am sitting in my home with a book before me" is a statement about my body. "I am reflecting on the relation between body and soul" is a statement about my soul. But clearly the word "I" means after all the same thing in both cases —me. True, this "I" is presented in two different senses, in one case spatially as my body in a certain place, in the other case as my reflecting soul. But my naïve consciousness of myself identifies as a matter of course what is presented to me in the two senses. In order to achieve the same identification philosophically, we must work out concepts that allow us to conceive at one and the same time both the difference in presentation and the identity of the given object. To this end I want to insert here a few remarks on the concept of identity.

The equation $x = x$, called by philosophers the law of identity, implies nothing. The concept of identity assumes importance only when we identify what is different, that is, when we write $x = y$. What does this mean? x and y are different signs. These signs, taken as letters, are not identical. But what they signify is identical. The equation states that x and y are signs for the same thing. The same distance may be measured in meters or in feet, and it is approximately correct to say 3 m = 10 ft. In this case, the identity is merely a consequence of a convention about measurements. But it may also be that the identification contains a new insight. In the Middle Ages, people knew that a certain country called India could be reached by the caravan route through Persia. Vasco da Gama sailed around the Cape of Good Hope and came to a country he called India. He identified the country he had reached by ship with the other one that had been known to be accessible by caravan route—and he was right. But his identification was not a matter of course, it contained an insight. Columbus crossed the Atlantic Ocean and found a country he identified with India—and he was wrong, for he had discovered America. Generally, the right to make the identification cannot be derived from either of the two routes. But if we dare make the identification, it opens the door to new insights and thereby to its own verification.

It is in this sense that I want to assert: Body and soul are not two substances but one. They are man becoming aware of himself in two different ways. To support my assertion I am appealing first to naïve common speech which says "I" for both body and soul. I believe that in this usage there is expressed a more genuine knowledge than in dualistic thinking which is committed to the two isolated methods of inquiry. I cannot attempt here to justify in detail the identification of body and soul, and so to indicate its exact meaning. That would lead us into the very depths of philosophy. But I wish to add a few explanations. If the identification is of value, it must be able to give us an insight into the problem why there are several approaches in the first place—just as we finally learned to trace both the caravan route and the sea way to India on a single map. I believe that body and soul do not constitute an absolute and original duality. Rather, they seem to me to be one of several possible divisions that arise in reality because of that polarity which I have called, vaguely enough, the contrast of subject and object.

Objectifying knowledge is self-oblivious. In the act of knowing I come to know the object, but I do not at the same time come to know the subject, myself. The eye does not see itself, the spotlight stands in the dark. If I am to see myself, a special, new act, a reflection of the light upon myself is needed. My body and my soul are two steps in this series of reflections.

The first level of objects we encounter are the things in space. On this level, subject and object are physically separate. The star, the stone, the animal, they are "there." But now I discover among the bodies one that is I. We can observe this discovery in children. The eye sees the hand, the hand touches the eye. I am a thing in space. The physical "I" has been discovered.

But I am not only the hand that is seen, or the eye that is touched—I am also the eye that sees and the hand that touches. I am sense perception, emotion of the soul, thought process. I am not only body, I am also soul—

perhaps soul first of all. The psychic "I" has been discovered.

I can turn the psychic "I" likewise into an object of
objectifying knowledge. I can practice psychology. But
any knowledge, including psychological knowledge, is
the knowledge gained by a subject. I can reflect upon
this subject, not as I know it through psychic experience,
but as the logical prerequisite that makes knowledge at
all possible. I can practice transcendental philosophy like
Kant and the idealists. The transcendental "I" has been
discovered.

But transcendental philosophy may be asked the question that Kierkegaard raised against Hegel: "Where do
you stand, you, a man who like a god philosophizes about
the absolute? You measure existence by the standards of
your thoughts. Before one can think, one must first exist.
What are the standards by which your existence is measured?" The existential "I," has been re-discovered.

Here I stop. Those who think their way through the
series of possible reflections must feel like one who in
a dream is plunging down a bottomless winding stair.
Every new step reveals that all preceding steps have told
of man only what is not essential. And yet he feels that
in each step the essence of man was implied. This is the
feeling I want to convey with the identification of subject and object. The physical, the psychic, the transcendental, and the existential "I" are not four different things,
they are only the signposts on four different roads that
I may follow to reach myself. They are the same "I." By
the identification of the stages through which I pass with
every turn, the winding spiral turns into a circle, the

bottomless plunge into a movement that returns into itself. And we must follow through this movement, not
just in our thoughts but also in our life. The demands
that this will make on us we shall be able to understand
only after we have spoken of the historic character of
man.

I want to devote the rest of this chapter to the history
of the soul in animals. It may be objected immediately
that by its very nature this history is unknown to us; that
we know the behavior, but never the soul of animals; that
in matters of the soul we know in reality only what we
know about ourselves, and that we draw conclusions
about the soul of even our closest fellow-men only by
way of analogy.

I consider this opinion epistemologically false. It was
not just a chance remark when I said at the outset of this
chapter that the soul is known to us as the "I," the "thou,"
and the "we." I believe that these three modes of knowing
the soul are all equally genuine. And I hope in this chapter at least to intimate that even from the purely scientific
point of view their equal genuineness must in fact be expected. But so much is certain, that we know the "thou"
in many cases far less well than the "I," particularly when
the "thou" is an animal. Therefore, I shall for the time
being proceed along the path that is considered orthodox
in natural science, and present animal psychology as the
study not of the animals' soul, but of their behavior. If
the identification of the physical and the psychic "I" is
justified, then those who are capable of perceiving matters
of the soul will be able to discern them in the behavior.

Animal psychology knows two fundamentally different forms of animal behavior: on the one hand, instinctive or inborn behavior, acquired and intelligent behavior on the other. I shall begin by following the analysis of instinctive actions as given by Konrad Lorenz.

"Instinct" is a short expression for the so far not analyzed complex of causes of what is called an instinctive action. We may leave open for the moment whether we wish to interpret instinct physically or psychically. What we observe is merely the behavior of the animal, that is, the instinctive action. An instinctive action may be defined as being analogous, in point of time, to what the organ is in point of space and matter. Just as the animal grows certain organs, without intent on its part and merely because of its heredity, so it also grows the faculty of using these organs. We know instinctive action also in man. The infant needs not only mouth, food pipe, and stomach in order to survive, but also the inborn faculties of suckling and swallowing. However, not every use of an organ is instinctive. We shall call instinctive only a sequence of motions that occurs with an inborn coordination of all its components, independently of training or understanding. That there are such inborn schemes of behavior is no more of a miracle than that there are organs at all. If natural selection has been able to bring forth differentiated organs, it must also have been able to produce similarly differentiated uses for them.

An inborn faculty does not necessarily have to be at the animal's command from the first day on. Inborn organs, too, often develop only when a certain stage in life has been reached. We shall call a faculty inborn if it develops independently of the experiences of the individual. Much of what we take for learned behavior is inborn in this sense. Young pigeons have been raised in narrow tubes where they could not open their wings. During the stage of life when pigeons usually learn to fly, one of them was released every day. The last pigeon to be released could fly as well after a few hours as the one that had been released first and had had twenty days in which to "learn." What seemed to be a learning process was merely the premature use of a not yet fully developed inborn faculty.

Instinct is blind. As a rule it is set off by a stimulus that is both very simple and very specific. The stimulus must fit into the animal's inborn scheme of reactions as the key fits into the lock. If the stimulus arises, the animal performs the instinctive action. The biological, objective purpose remains a secret to the animal. This becomes evident when, because of an insufficient stimulus, the instinctive action is interrupted shortly before its biological purpose has been achieved, or when the action is performed fully in cases in which it is senseless or even damaging. A well-known illustration is offered by the long trains of processionary caterpillars in which each animal attaches its head to the tail-end of the one preceding it, and then merely follows after. If the leader of such a train gets into a hole from which it cannot escape, the entire train stops and may remain stopped until all the caterpillars have starved to death. I have seen such trains of dried-up processionary caterpillars. Man has even succeeded by certain contraptions in guiding the leader of such a train behind the rear caterpillar. The leader attached itself to the rear animal. Then the procession went on in a circle until all had perished.

For some instinctive actions there exists something like an internal pressure which grows if the action has not been performed for some time, and which is relieved when the action is performed. In such cases, the stimulus looses its edge by repetition. Conversely, long failure of the stimulus to occur may result in spontaneous, pointless action. For example, a starling had been raised in a room that contained no insects and no other birds. This bird had never seen an insect hunt. One day it took aim at some imaginary point in the room, flew up to it, pecked, tossed its head sideways as starlings do to kill a captured insect, swallowed, and returned contentedly to its perch.

If it is permissible for once to ask what may be the subjective correlative of the instinctive action, it is obviously not the notion of the purpose that is ascribed to the action by the objective observer, but rather a compulsion or a pleasure connected with the action itself. We human beings can add in thought the purpose to our instinctive actions. In fact, we experience daily the conflict between the two kinds of motivation, for understanding does not wipe out a connection between action and pleasure that has been practiced through millions of years of selection. But so far as the mechanism of selection is concerned, it is not the pleasure that counts but only the objective purpose of the action. An animal species is fit for life if it accomplishes the purpose of its actions, at least by and large.

The instinctive actions that govern the social behavior of animals develop in a special fashion. All other instincts have to react to those often quite undifferentiated stimuli that the environment happens to provide. Social animals react to fellow-animals of the same species. Thus, the stimulus itself may vary here throughout the evolution of the species: both lock and key may adapt themselves each to the other. For instance, even secondary marks of sex call forth erotic reactions. This often makes possible selective mating among closely related species. Ducks are born with the knowledge what kind of band the drake must wear around its neck to be the right one for them. The stimulus may also be itself an instinctive action: The warning cry starts the flight of the herd. In many cases, the rudiment of an instinctive action which itself no longer serves the original purpose becomes the prompting "symbol." Certain kinds of geese, for instance, invite their fellows to fly off by a head movement that itself was once the beginning of flight. We are reminded that organs and instinctive actions do not have a "natural" purpose that is fixed once and for all. To produce sounds, crickets use their already existing wing-cases, mammals their already existing breathing organs. The new purpose may turn into the only purpose: the swim bladder has become the lung. Thus, an organ or sequence of actions may acquire the sole purpose of communicating with fellow-animals. Among the most striking examples for this are the gestures of submission. In a fight between two turkeys, the loser can stop the battle by pressing itself flat upon the ground. In this position it is entirely defenseless against further attack. But in the winner, this very gesture calls forth an unsurmountable inhibition against continuing the fight. Having achieved the socially superior position, the winner is forced by nature to be generous, and to spare the opponent's life. The value of this performance for the preservation of the species is obvious. But only the fellow-animal of the same species, with its inborn understanding of the gesture of submission, reacts to that gesture. In a fight between turkey and peacock the gesture is of no avail. The peacock will go on hacking away at the prostrate turkey, and the turkey is so firmly locked in its attitude that it allows itself to be hacked to death.

I believe these facts throw new light on the question whether the soul of the "thou" is immediately known to us. Animals have learned their expressive motions not just within the span of their individual life. Both the expressive motion and the understanding of it are inborn. It is not the individual but the species that accomplished what was needed to achieve communication. Since instinct is older than intelligence, we might also say: understanding is older than thought. Consequently, there must be an understanding that requires no analogy from the "I" to the "thou." We know this sort of understanding even in man. Before the baby can talk, it returns a smile for a smile. A woman senses it when a man woos her. True, the sureness of nature that is in this sort of understanding is also what sets its limits. There is no conclusion from the "I" to the "thou," and hence no possibility for the "I" to imagine itself in the position of the "thou." This understanding merely means the faculty to act out, spontaneously and correctly, the proper role of the "I" in the common game. Of the role of the "thou" only the cue words are really known. That is why understanding of this sort is generally confined to fellows of the same species. The peacock no longer understands the gesture of the turkey.

Instinctive understanding can be deceived by simple contraptions, and paralyzed by a small variation in circumstances. A songbird will feed the young cuckoo in the nest, but will let its own brood starve to death if the cuckoo has pushed them out—for the brood must sit in the nest to be worth feeding. If we put the young ones back into the nest they will be cared for with affection, and will again be fed. We human beings often act no better when one of our social taboos has been violated, though as a rule these taboos are not inborn.

Instinctive understanding, therefore, is not infallible—like every instinct, it is blind to its own nature. But it is the raw material with which the structure of conscious understanding is built. What we know of our fellow-men is communicated through spontaneous or conventional expression, through gesture, speech, or writing. The basis of the expression, however, is instinctive understanding. Certainly, our knowledge of the "thou" is subject to errors, but so is our knowledge of the "I." Which of the two is more difficult to understand, the "I" or the "thou," this question remains unanswered even in the highest stages of our knowledge of the soul. The "I" is distinguished merely by the fact that it can be experienced without there being any need of expressions perceived by the senses.

The road to intelligence leads through individual experience. An increasing differentiation of the instincts does not lead to intelligence, it renders intelligence superfluous. Conversely, intelligence presupposes gaps in the bonds of instinct, in its higher degrees it presupposes in fact a decay of the instincts. The beginnings of intelligence are found in self-training by experience. Ravens building their nests will start out by picking up just any object—a straw, a pebble, a piece of glass—and attempt to fasten it in the spot where the nest is to be built. After a time, they lose the habit of all objects except those that stay in place when the nest is subjected to a peculiar sideways strain by the pushing and shaking of construction. We hardly may assume that the raven knows it is trying to build a nest. But the satisfaction that comes when the object stays fastened to the nest, seems to be inducement enough for the bird to perform this self-training. Now let us compare the raven to other birds that are born even with the exact knowledge of the materials from which they must build their nests. Such birds spare themselves many fruitless attempts. But if they do not find their specific material, for instance, certain grasses, they can build no nest at all. The raven, by virtue of the gap in its chain of instincts, is capable of adapting itself to many different environments. Instincts may be extraordinarily complicated, but they are rigid. Learned actions or intelligent actions are more primitive, but also more adaptable.

A learned action is one that is not inborn, but is performed like an instinctive action in consequence of a certain stimulus, yet without an understanding of the reasons why it is successful. The source of learning, in most cases, is self-training by trial and error, or perhaps an already "learned" fellow. We conclude that we are dealing with an intelligent action when essentially new situations are being mastered, situations that no trial and error could conquer. Thus, Koehler observed chimpanzees using a bamboo stick to pull into the cage a fruit out of their reach, and even sticking two bamboos one into the other when one of them was not long enough. What is inborn in these cases is not the sequence of actions, but the faculty to develop the habit of a sequence of actions, and to go through it spontaneously and correctly. We call such faculties the ability to learn and intelligence. Little is known so far of their evolution among animals, and particularly of the forces that have driven this evolution forward.

XI

Man: Outer History

I BEGIN to talk of man only with reluctance. I am too well aware how inadequate is what I can say on the subject. The nature and history of man are matters on which there are not just two or three but countless conflicting opinions. And here the conflict concerns not only the right answers, but even the right way of asking questions. I have formed an opinion about the relative importance of the questions, but answers I can give only in a few cases, and then only gropingly.

Still, it seems to me that I cannot remain silent about man. We started out with the question what man is, and only in this question will the circle of our reflections close. In one sense, man is the final stage in the evolution of nature. But—we ourselves are man, in this very sense. Only after we have pursued the history of nature up to man do we become aware that by inquiring into nature we are inquiring into ourselves. It also becomes clear that it makes good sense to take the roundabout way over nature when we are pressed hard by the problem what we ourselves are. In this chapter, I shall consider man as a being who has originated in nature, and from the viewpoints we have gained in the preceding chapter. In the final chapter I shall talk of man in the way in which he has immediate knowledge of himself.

I do not see how we can escape the conclusion that man is physically descended from beings whom biology must classify as apes. However, these our ancestors can probably not be found among the ape species living today. The present species have most likely developed past the point that branched off toward man. Fundamentally, this changes nothing in our descent from the apes.

Man is distinguished from the apes even physically by two new acquisitions: the upright walk, and the size of his brain. Both achievements are probably among the material conditions on which his mental development depends. That the large brain is needed for thinking seems clear. The upright walk, in turn, frees the hand. Now the hand no longer serves for locomotion, but for arts and crafts. How much the hand has shaped our way of thinking is still shown in our language: we "grasp" an idea.

Man is physically a very unspecialized being. He eats plants and animals. He walks, climbs, and swims. Specialized animals surpass him in every one of his various skills, but none seem to excel him in their combination. We are given to admire instances of high specialization. But they are always adapted to very specific conditions of life, and when these conditions disappear they perish with them. It is probable that all upward evolution begins with the less specialized members of a species. In some beings such as man, lack of specialization is in fact the distinctive characteristic on which success depends. Lack of specialization does not mean a shortcoming, it means many-sidedness. Even physically, man can perform a greater variety of tasks than any animal. With the possible exception of the elephant, there is hardly an animal that could carry a suitcase for five miles. If it has the strength, it lacks the organ of grasping. Man is not restricted to one climate, as are the anthropoids. And among the races of man, those least specialized in point of climate are again the most successful.

Man could be called the specialist of hand and brain. But this would mean using the word "specialization" in a rather doubtful sense, since those highly differentiated organs, hand and brain, are organs precisely of many-sidedness. Instincts are specializations upon a particular sequence of actions. Man is comparatively poor in instinctive ties. This leaves him free to act in accordance with changing situations, and even to try more than one course of action in the same situation. Step by step, man uses this freedom. First, he fills the sphere that instinct has left free, with actions he learns to perform without yet understanding them. In this sphere made unfree once more by such tradition, there must then grow the freedom of personal understanding. Human speech may serve to illustrate how the three elements, inborn, learned, and intelligent behavior, work together. The ability to produce sounds with our organs of speech, and to attach a meaning to the sounds, is inborn. The child learns his particular language—not his parentage, but the tradition in which he grows up determines language. Finally, what man expresses in his language is at least partially his own achievement.

Let us now look at the external framework of what

man calls world history. I shall limit myself to the sector that is closest to us, Europe and the old civilizations around the Mediterranean that have been Europe's teachers.

Man has developed in the Ice Age. This, I believe, is not just a coincidence. Rapid changes in the external conditions of life favor the advance of the species. And a deterioration in the circumstances of life as radical as the Ice Age must have placed on intelligence a far higher premium than the mild climate of the Tertiary that had gone before. I could well imagine that man went through the essential stages in his development just in those regions where the climate was unfavorable. Remains of prehistoric man are found in the Europe of the Ice Age, often close to the limits of the inhabitable zone.

To produce the human races seems to have taken tens of thousands of years. After the last great glaciation, man enters the period in which he has created nearly all of what we call civilization. At that moment mankind is already divided into the races we know today. The units we call peoples are more recent, racially mixed historical formations. The European peoples of today are even younger than the so-called Migration of Nations.

To be sure, the first high civilizations arose in the warm climate of Egypt, Mesopotamia, and India, or at least in the temperate climate of China. But it is doubtful whether the races that created those civilizations really had their origins in the same regions. We know of vast migrations in prehistoric times. It may be that the fight for life in the rough climates formed men strong both in body and in mind, though only milder climates allowed them to turn their gifts to anything beyond the bare fight for life. For the earliest times this may be beyond proof—it becomes obvious for the past four thousand years, since the entrance into history of the Indo-Europeans. Ever since then, the peoples of the north have migrated south, east, and west.

About 1800 B.C., their first assault rocks the empires of the Near East. The Hittites invade Babylonia, the Hyksos Egypt. The migration continues in waves. The Aryans conquer Iran and India, the Hellenes Greece, the Italians Italy. The Celts, the Germans push after. The Roman Empire, itself founded by Italians, for some centuries raises a barrier. Then follows the period called specifically the Migration of Nations. The movement continues through the Middle Ages. The German emperors reach over into Italy, the Vikings of the north found their realms in England and Normandy, Russia, and Sicily. In modern times the current turns west across the ocean, and east into the steppes of Southern Russia and Siberia.

Throughout these millenniums, the north has the greater strength, the south the higher civilization. But the truly creative zone appears to be the surf line that is cast up where the current of strength enters the regions of civilization. Old civilizations tend to grow tired, sheer strength consumes itself in battle, and only where they meet do they arouse each other to activity of the highest order. Just as fire, and life itself, is a process that consumes ever new substance, just so, it seems, ever new nations become the fuel of the fire of the mind.

The surf line slowly moves upstream toward the north. The reason is perhaps that a growing and expanding external civilization eases the fight for life until even in colder climates the mind is freed for other tasks. In the first millennium before Christ the surf line moves from the Near East to Greece, later it includes Italy. France rises after the Migration of Nations, Germany follows. England has her ascent in modern times, and today America and Russia announce their claims.

The image of the surf line expresses the supra-national continuity of the mind. Each single nation over which the surf line passes presents a different picture in which rise is followed by decline. Each single case has its peculiarities, yet in all of them are found some elements of the following evolutionary pattern:

At the beginning stands a long and stable period. Later generations will call it the Heroic Age. Its world of thought may be called mythical, its political condition is perhaps best described as aristocratic. Its art, though primitive in the eyes of later ages, is genuine.

Next, and most likely always after contact with culturally more advanced nations, begins a development which often fills the span of a thousand years. I can mention only a few of its countless characteristics. Mythical thought turns into rational thought, and in this change, too, the most productive moment is perhaps the moment of transition, the surf line. Art and philosophy flower in this period, political expansion usually goes hand in hand with an increase in intellectual power, or at least alternates with it.

Natural science, technology, and external civilization are a later stage. But even as the utmost is being accomplished in the mastery of life, there appear signs of decay. Now there is scepticism, and something which was impossible in the early era: sham art, *Kitsch*. One fine day, the people awakens to the fact that even politically it is no longer equal to the situation. Unnoticed by it, neighbors have grown up to be stronger than the people itself. These neighbors overrun the older civilization, learn from it, and fall into the same process.

The last remarks may have brought to mind the name of Spengler. I do not want to identify myself with any one of Spengler's statements. But it was Spengler who has secured attention for the doctrine of a law governing the rise and decline of civilizations. This doctrine, I believe, is worthy of our closest study.

This doctrine is the morphology of history. As such, it seems to me to express an indisputable though partial truth. But it is probably too narrow in three respects. Even as morphology, it is not the final answer. And then, it is merely a challenge for us to ask these two questions: what are the causes of history, and what is its meaning?

My remarks about the surf line were meant to stress another side of the morphology of history. The history of human civilization, seen from the view-point of a single nation or group of nations, may appear like a wave that merely rises and then sinks again. But as we survey all nations we see that the wave is moving along. It sinks in one place and rises in another. In its travel, the wave does not retain its form, rather it shows a consistent continuity of transformation, often interrupted yet always resumed. Homer, Socrates, Christ have so changed the world that to escape their effects, even by ignorance, would be next to impossible. Modern rationalism may be another such irreversible change. The movement is entering a new phase also in that today it covers the whole earth. So far, there have always been "young" nations, ready to snatch the torch from the older ones. Some day there will be no young nation left. The history of mankind, like every historic process, is unique and irreversible. Let it be repeated on another planet, or in the far-off future: in itself, it does not bear the marks of eternal duration, or of perpetual undulation.

We cannot hope to develop these first beginnings of a morphology into a convincing picture unless we inquire into the causes of history. The word "cause" in this context is ambiguous. Man may look on the life of his fellow from outside, as one looks on an event in nature, or he may see it from inside, such as his fellow himself experiences it. Man may state facts, or he may understand the other human being with that kind of understanding which exists in conversation, or in love. Accordingly, man will call the connection among facts, in the first case, their causal relation; in the second case, their meaning. Our desire to identify the subjective and objective sides of history makes us assume that both connections point toward one and the same thing, and this one thing is what I mean by the word cause. There is so far no other road to lead us closer to this cause than to round once again both halves of the circle. In this chapter I intend to pursue the problem of causal relation as far as I am able. In the final chapter I shall turn to the problem of meaning.

What are the causes of the movement of history? We begin by studying the picture of rise and decline as we see it in the various civilizations. We have before us here two movements, the rising, and the falling.

The rising movement is as intelligible—or as mysterious—as the rise of man himself. On the new levels of social order and of the mind, it follows the same path from simplicity to differentiation that we witness in the history of nature generally. The 19th century faith in progress spent itself in the contemplation of this phase. For the moment I shall not discuss it further. For I am convinced that we shall achieve a far profounder understanding of the driving force of the ascent if we first study the second phase, the decline.

When we speak of the decline of civilizations, we usually express ourselves in images borrowed from biology. We talk of old nations and dying civilizations. This imagery is often striking. We must be all the more careful to realize that so far we have no more than an image that we find difficult to understand in causal terms. Already in our earlier discussion of star systems I explained that the development from the creative absence of differentiation to the growth of forms, and on to the rigor of death, is characteristic not alone of organic life, but of the historic structure of the world throughout. We are certain to find this same structure wherever we are able to observe a historical process unfolding without outside interference. It is bound to hold true for a biological individual no less than for a civilization. And this fact shows just how little specifically biological substance there is in the comparison between a civilization or a people, and an individual. The remarks at the close of the ninth chapter might perhaps allow us to understand why the individual grows old. But if those remarks are true, then it may be said, speaking purely in biological terms, that the individual grows old and dies in order that the species may stay young and life may go on. Ants have existed for a hundred million years, and up to this day they have lost nothing of their vitality. Why then should a people develop like an individual rather than like a species? Biologically, it seems at first past understanding that peoples should grow old in a mere few thousand years. In other words: While the morphological law of the development of a civilization is perfectly intelligible once we assume the natural life span of a civilization to be a mere few thousand years, nothing in the biological analogy allows us to understand at all why that life span should be so short.

I believe it is quite possible that the aging of peoples is due to a change in the biological heritage. If so, the change is not a primary phenomenon but rather the consequence of processes for which the history of organic life offers hardly any analogy. We must find out what these processes are.

Man's freedom from the bonds of instinct is both his strength and his danger. He can rise above inborn patterns of behavior. But when he does so, his actions have no longer the assurance of inborn behavior. Man experiments, and his experiments fail often enough. He is himself something of an experiment of nature, and who would predict whether the experiment will on the whole succeed? A certain stability exists in man's early, mythical stage, when the rule of deep-grown traditions keeps from the individual's arbitrary fancy the areas left open by inborn patterns. The actual break-through into intellectual self-reliance and rational civilization, however, is a revolution. Through it man enters an essentially unstable phase, and so far there is not a sign of a new stability toward which the transformation might be tending. Measured against the time scales of the earth, the millenniums of human history are the sudden flash of a new possibility, a lightning-swift journey into the unknown. To view it with detachment is difficult for us who ourselves are the travellers.

Certain remarks of Lorenz may guide us in our study of the effects that intellectual liberation had upon the factors which once endowed life with stability. We may leave open here a question that Lorenz treats as settled in most cases. He believes the stabilizing factors to be mostly inborn. But the effects he describes would appear in almost the same fashion if those factors were in part traditional. The difference assumes importance only when we look for a cure, since it is easier to re-create tradition than biological heritage. But these practical problems would lead beyond the scope of my work. A therapy would demand a more specific diagnosis than I can give in these pages.

Lorenz compares the effect of civilization on society with the familiar spectacle of the domestication of animals. The qualities that offer an advantage in the fight for life to an animal in its natural surroundings, are different from those for a domesticated animal. The animal in the wilderness is surrounded with dangers. It must have keen senses, readiness for fight or sudden flight, great care of its brood, and stable ways of social behavior. Among wild geese, the making of a marriage requires that both partners possess a large number of very specific qualities, and perform a certain rite of selection. The marriage so contracted lasts for life, and the young are raised with care and protected with passion. Domesticated animals are relieved of such tasks by man. For them, the opponent in the fight for life is no longer a world of enemies all around, but the envious fellow animal in the manger. Varieties that in the wilderness would be doomed to extinction, can now survive and multiply. The sharply defined, harmoniously balanced mental and physical make-up of the wild animal gives way to wide variations in all characteristics. Overly large and undersized freak forms, dachshund legs, drooping bellies, and pug-faces make their appearance. The domestic goose knows nothing of the strict marriage code of the wild goose, and mating and family sense fall apart. In this condition propagation is most rapid. If domesticated and wild geese are kept in captivity under identical conditions, the domesticated geese will soon outnumber the others by far. But only the wild geese will survive a hard winter without man's protection. To win out in the fight for life, the domesticated animal needs only to "feed and breed, promiscuously and without measure" (Lorenz).

Animals of this description arouse our spontaneous contempt. What we commonly call "beastly" are not at all the traits of the wild beast but those of the domesticated one. Why the contempt? From the point of view of efficiency it is a misunderstanding. The domesticated animal is perfectly adapted to its environment. The majority of the large animals on earth today are domesticated, so successful is their behavior. Man himself does not want a noble pig, he wants a fat pig. He values animals by their capacity to become his slaves. But for his coats-of-arms he has chosen, not the pig, but lion and eagle. Here man judges the animal as if it were human, and there is deep within him a loathing for the traits of domestication in man himself. This loathing is a protection against that self-domestication which is one of the consequences of civilization. I mean to discuss not the physical consequences of civilization, but only the intellectual ones. They grow out of a twofold effect: On the one hand, civilization removes dangers. On the other, it creates new ones.

As man's surroundings become less of a danger, and as his numbers increase, fellow-man becomes the chief opponent in the fight for life. Both inborn and learned social behavior patterns, once necessities that alone made man's existence possible, now turn into obstacles to the advance of the individual. Lorenz is probably right in assuming that most of our ethical and aesthetic value judgments—our high regard for fidelity, maternal love, and everything that we call good and beautiful—are inborn traits. But the result would hardly be different if they were acquired. For all these traits restrain the individual in favor of the community. In the beginning, this community is usually small. Individuals who act differently are damaging to the community, and are cast out. Then the civilized state relieves all small communities of the necessity to defend themselves. Yet much time must go by before man realizes what kind of behavior is damaging to the civilized state. In the new manner of the fight for life, an individual's moral inferiority means greater opportunities for him. The sort of man who is not patently criminal, but base and unrestrained in small matters, that is the sort who gets ahead. But he cannot maintain the social order which begot him. If he seizes power and holds it, the structure collapses.

Then there are also the new dangers of civilization against which man is protected by no instinct. It is well known that animals of prey do not attack their own kind. They have to have an instinct restraining them, else they would kill each other off in short order. But defenseless animals like rabbits or turtle doves, when confined together, often destroy each other in the most cruel fashion. They have no restraint against an action that hardly ever happens in the wilderness where flight is open at any moment. Man is by nature not an animal of prey. Without a weapon it would be difficult for him to kill his fellows. And this is why he is by nature almost completely without restraint once he has invented weapons. The ethics of the weapon, the ethics of all power over our fellows, is the crucial problem of our growth into human beings. In early history, the code of honor of the noblemen and freemen bearing arms created a traditional order that was still barely tolerable. With the advance of civilization, the problem has grown more acute, and who could claim that we have solved it?

What are we to do?

As we become aware of the dangers of civilization, we are tempted to wish ourselves back into the past. I believe this wish is delusive. True, a comparison with the past may tell us much about what is wrong with the present. But, first, we cannot return to past conditions. History is irreversible. The hollowness of every restoration shows that there is no lasting remedy in the re-establishment of by-gone forms without the spontaneous forces that once created them. And secondly, that very same past was itself unstable, and the direction in which it was tending was this our present. Pre-historic conditions, when the course of history had not yet begun, are neither accessible nor desirable for us. We should not forget that the decay of instincts that casts us into danger, is at the same time the condition on which depends our growth into human beings. Man is an experiment that cannot be interrupted half-way. It has begun, now it must be completed.

There is the pessimistic view that utter ruin is the only outcome possible. Among all the ideas I have so far presented, there is not one that could disprove this view. Even in the world of biology, only the old is stable. The new is always a gamble which is lost often, if not most often. We know new forms that, at the outset, are successful in their fight for life, and yet in the end bring on their own destruction. The beast of prey that multiplies more quickly than its prey is an example. Such an animal will go on spreading until all its prey is eaten up, then it will starve to death. How can we prove that man is not like this animal?

But ruin is a certainty for any being that forsakes itself. If we do not want to forsake ourselves, we must impel the force that struck the wound to help in the healing. Man has lost the ties of instinct, and in return he has received the power of mind to grasp his own situation. Instinct was secure, but blind. Thought is exposed to danger, but it sees. Could not at least a few men see the danger, and see the cure? And then, would they not have to do all they can, with the superiority lent by insight, to see to it that the cure is followed?

I shall not dwell on what the cure might be. My diagnosis, as I said before, is not precise enough. But I must try to define the human attitude that alone would entitle us even to search for the cure. We have come back now to the point from which we started. Knowledge is power, but power may in the end destroy itself. That broad and penetrating knowledge I have called insight might give to those who have it perhaps the broadest power. What manner of men would they have to be so that we should be willing to grant them the use of such power?

Our inquiry has gone beyond the confines of objectifying science. Even while we were studying man as one of nature's beings, we were unable to forget that we ourselves are this being. We cannot hope to find an adequate answer unless we ask explicitly in what way man, since time out of mind, has knowledge of himself.

XII

Man: Inner History

M AN does not know himself as a being that one could study with detachment. He always finds himself faced with demands made on him, demands that he must follow or reject. Misery, anguish and hope, love and hate, custom and conscience, fellow-man and God make demands on him. Much of man's knowledge of himself can be expressed properly not as a statement, but only as an imperative. While I am writing these lines, I can exempt neither myself nor my reader from these imperatives. I can write only if I assume my reader to be subject to imperatives, and if I were not subject to them myself I should not be writing.

But it is impossible to stop with the mere demands. They often contradict one another. For they have fallen into confusion in the course of history, and the trouble of our age is just that we can no longer tell which call to follow, which to reject. The aim of thinking in the circle of subject and object is to employ what inner coherence science still possesses, to guide us in the realm of imperatives. Our method is intended to lend consistency to the subjective side, and to the objective side, substance.

We must proceed perhaps as follows: Our starting point

in every case must be the immediate experience man has of himself. This experience takes most often the form of an imperative. Like all immediate experience it is isolated, it is full of seeming contradictions, perhaps it is even un-intelligible—but there it is. Our hardest task will be, with-out getting confused by theories, to see experience in all purity, even if it does not happen to coincide with our own most personal experience. Next, we shall have to interpret it by a comparison with the objective informa-tion about man. This objective information—treating of man as a being of nature, a being of history, an object of philosophy—constitutes theory. It is orderly and intel-ligible, but it may be wrong. It needs incessant checking against immediate experience. After all, theory must serve the life it interprets. For all our decisions about ourselves are ultimately made in the realm of those demands I men-tioned at the outset. Theory does not relieve us of deci-sions—all it can do is show us the consequences of our decision for one course of action or another.

First let me clarify by an example the methodolog-ical position into which we shall be led. I choose a prob-lem which, to be sure, has already been talked about more than it deserves. But it happens to be closely tied up with a confusion in identifying the subjective and the objective. I mean the problem of the freedom of will.

My freedom to do within certain limits what I have resolved to do is an immediate experience. Whether or not to call on a friend tonight, that is something I have to think about precisely because I am free to do it or not to do it. I can be expected to obey traffic regulations be-cause it is known that I can follow them if I want to.

Throughout our thinking everywhere there are ideas that make sense only with reference to such freedom. It is the logical basis for the imperative mood in thought and speech. Demands can be made only on a will known to be free. In contrasting subject and object, we ascribe to the object not freedom but, at best, only some unpredictable behavior, while the freedom to inquire and manipulate at will belongs logically among the defining characteristics of the subject endowed with understanding. The very concept of the law of nature requires that he who conducts the experiment be free to repeat at will the original conditions.

The subject itself, however, is often considered a special object that is merely one of the links in a chain of causation. If this is the case, then freedom of will is really only the freedom to do what I have decided to do. But it remains open why I decide to do this rather than that. Those who believe that every event is causally determined will then assume that my decision, too, has been determined by some cause, although the cause remains unknown to me. Thus, my will would "in reality" be unfree.

I do not know whether this theory is correct. I merely want to emphasize that it is a theory and not a matter of experience. It represents a challenge for future empirical research. Let the determining factors of our actions be brought to light, and we shall believe in them. But the freedom which makes the subject what it is, that freedom is a matter of experience. I do not think that the admission of freedom as a matter of experience is in itself enough to refute determinism. For it has no reply to the assertion that the determining factors are merely unknown to us. But conversely, the revelation of some such unknown motives would not invalidate the admission in the sense in which it is intended. No science of psychology can take from me the burden of the decisions I must make in life. As long as the uncertainty of the future is not in fact removed, a being who says "I" must make his choices, whether he believes them to be predetermined or not.

There is an objective counterpart to this subjective experience of freedom, which can likewise be considered without reference to the theory of determinism. That is the freedom from the compulsion of instinct. The completely instinctive action is predetermined. If we subject an animal to a certain stimulus we can predict its reaction. We experience within ourselves the lack of freedom at those moments when we are at the mercy of our instincts. But rational action is free. Even in the case of an animal acting rationally, we are unable to predict which of several alternatives it will choose. For here a choice is made within the individual, and no heredity nor tradition relieves it of that choice. If there are any determining motives, they are at any rate essentially unknown at the moment the choice is made. It seems to me that all theories of indeterminism are based on this subjective experience of these objective facts.

Thus the idea of subjective freedom is threatened not by the theories of determinism, but rather by our own immediate experience of the absence of freedom, an experience we have, for instance, when we are acting under the compulsion of instinct. The most important experiences of this sort are made in the sphere of religion. I experience that I cannot do good even if I want to. I experience that if I do good, I do not do so out of my own power—I undergo it as an act of grace. These are the realities that lead beyond the idea of freedom. But they cannot be put into words unless the idea of freedom has first been presupposed.

We must now turn to the imperatives that determine man's life. They have grown out of religion. Hence, we must turn to religion. True, there is such a thing as pure ethics, freed of all religious bonds. But it never comes at the beginning. It grows out of a certain manner in which rational thinking comes to terms with the imperatives of religion. We can do justice to pure ethics only if we first understand religion.

To talk of religion is more difficult than to talk of anything else in all of human life. It must be so—for how could we hope to resolve into concepts of thought the very things on which our existence and our thoughts depend? Men who knew what God is, also knew that of God one can speak only with fear and trembling.

But since I have begun to speak I must formulate our difficulty more exactly. It is impossible to assign its proper place to an experience that one could not have himself. In the sphere of religion, this is to say: It is impossible to understand the nature of a god in whom one could not believe. For the religious experience knows itself to be experience of the divine. And it believes in the divine through experiencing it. This is where almost all reasoning about religion comes to grief. Men who are firmly committed to a religious faith can talk about their god as he appears within his own domain. They can proclaim their god. But mankind has had many gods, and to the man who is committed in faith, all other gods will remain strangers—and therefore, the world of religion as a whole will remain strange to him. Those not committed in faith, on the other hand, may well be able to see the whole of the world of religion from the outside, as an object; but its inwardness, and that means its essence, will as a rule remain totally unknown to them. Is it possible to turn in faith to several gods at once? Is it possible to believe, and to think objectively at the same time? With the exception of a few profound thinkers, true theology until today has remained intolerant almost of necessity, and the true science of religion has almost of necessity remained on the surface.

Until lately, it has been possible to leave things at such a pass. Religion is older than rational thought, and has not had too great a need of the assistance of rational thought. Scepticism has been the privilege of a few men of learning who could survive because around them stood a world of faith unshaken. Today, scepticism has entered the masses, and has rocked the foundations of their order of life. It is the men of learning who are frightened now. They fear that the surrender of religious immediacy has been too high a price for rational thought. But we cannot go back. There is no honest retreat from rational thought into naïve belief. It is an old saying that the first sip from the cup of knowledge cuts us off from God—but in the bottom of the cup God waits for those who seek him. If this is so, then thought can find a road that will lead onward to religious truth, and that is the only road worth seeking. If it is not so, then our world will base its hopes on religion in vain.

We shall not conquer our difficulties by belittling them. If we are to arrive at an understanding we must stress them. They will stand out more sharply if we recall the religious experiences of transcendence, and of the battle of the gods.

The understanding of transcendence differs among religions. They share in common the idea that the god is beyond the reach of human power. The god is not in the hands of man, man is in the hands of the god. The god is not always and at will accessible to man. He reveals himself where he pleases, when he pleases, as he pleases. The images in which men have conceived this may be to us no more than parables. But the matter itself is one of experience. It is possible to reject religion, but it is not possible to accept religion and at the same time to strike out of it the transcendent godhead.

These powers, higher than man, further exist in religious experience as battling, disunited powers. Polytheism, to be sure, is the worship of several gods at once. Zeus and Apollo, or Wotan and Thor, may be worshipped simultaneously. But in the same religions we find the mythical images of the battle between groups of gods. There is Wotan, but beside him there is Loki. Then Balder is slain, and the Twilight of the Gods must come. Chronos unmanned Uranos and devoured his own children, then Zeus overthrew him. There are historical events corresponding to these images. The Olympic religion had won out over the older chthonian gods, and then it had in turn to yield to Christianity. Christianity considered the older gods as demons, and this, I believe, shows a truer appraisal of their divine rank than the later humanistic harmonizations which avoided the conflict by understanding both sides in a sense that neglected their essence. Christianity has again a mythical image of the god-opposing force in Lucifer, and an image of its own disputed future in Anti-Christ. And indeed, some modern movements have raised new meanings to religious rank—Reason, Freedom, Equality, Blood—although no longer in the mythical form of divine persons.

A man who is committed in faith can dismiss all other gods as idols. It would be wrong to try robbing him of his certainty. His horizon may be narrow, still in some point he possesses immediate experience. This alone raises him above any mere scepticism. But we have all been touched by scepticism. Do we believe in transcendence? Can we reconcile it with the battle of the gods? I do not want to discuss these questions in general, but shall concern myself now with those gods in whom men have actually believed.

I shall bypass the early gods of nature, and speak of a circle of gods that represents to us already something of the highest in human life: the gods of the Olympic religion of the Greeks. They have human shape. Yet they are transcendent, although not in the same sense as the God of Christianity later on. They do not live among us like men. They dwell beyond the regions we can enter, in Olympus, a heavenly abode. Yet they are not absolutely beyond reach. In sacrifice, in prayer, in an unexpected turn of fortune, in dreams, or in a sudden dread that befalls us, the god is present. But he reveals himself when and where he pleases, not when and where man pleases.

I am giving the floor immediately to rationalistic criticism of religion, such as even the late Greeks themselves raised against their own gods. All of us are convinced of this much: nowhere in physical space are there such man-like beings as Zeus, or Athene, nor have they ever existed anywhere, barring lifeless statues. And yet, these mythical images express great and inescapable realities. But the realm in which they have reality is not the material outer world, it is the human soul itself. And there, in the human soul, what are they? What now of their transcendence? Is this transcendence not merely a mistaken outward projection of something in ourselves?

There is a simple first approach to the reality of the gods. It is the doctrine that the gods embody qualities, forces, situations in man's life. Ares is battle, and the fire and fury of battle. Aphrodite is beauty that arouses love. Apollo is the spirit of divination, of art, and of understanding. Zeus is dominion, order, the kingdom.

But why did these human qualities have to be embodied in gods? I would say first that the mythical thought of religion is older than philosophical abstraction. At the outset, man can conceive of the abstract only by way of a concrete form. The path from many beautiful persons to the abstract concept of beauty as such leads through the concrete image of beauty as such: Aphrodite.

Yet the gods are not concepts in concrete garb. Aphrodite was addressed in prayer. There are many areas where we may no longer agree with the men who thought in mythical terms—but we will have to grant them that they knew whether they were committing an absurdity. And to pray to a mere concept is absurd, even if it is concealed in the statue of a god. Religious experience affirms that more is at stake. The gods are not concepts, they are powers. In fact, they are the ruling powers of man's life.

But what are powers? How can we think of them in non-mythical and yet adequate terms? This is a central problem in the understanding of religion. I can offer no more than the beginnings of an explanation.

Power is what is mighty. "Mighty" is related to "make," and to what "might be," what is possible. The future is what is possible. Power has to do with the future. External power holds future events in its hands. In this sense, too, the gods have been considered powerful. But more important, they are internal powers. We must remember that the gods have human shape. The rationalistic explanation quickly comes to mind that man has made god in his own image. The Bible has it the other way: God created man in His image, as His image He created him. This, I believe, is the profounder truth. In non-mythical terms: the image in which God appears to man does not show what man is but what he might be. It is the image of man's potentiality of being, that which determines his life. This potentiality is for man a power, not a concept. Concepts we have of things past, things we have mastered. But this potentiality is what we have not yet mastered. Man is not master over it, it is master over him. It may be up to us to fulfill this potentiality, or to fail it—but to choose it is not up to us. How it happens that the potentiality reveals itself to us, that remains hidden from us. It challenges us, and our life is obedience to it, or flight from it.

I do not say that this image of the objective potentiality exhausts the idea of divinity. The metaphysics behind the fact that the divine reveals itself to us in this fashion, that is something I do not dare touch upon. But I believe that this image is the form in which we can best manage to grasp in thought what we know of the divine. Perhaps we can thus understand at once both the transcendence and the multitude of the gods, and with it also the combination in religion of the supra-historical with the historical. In different ages, among different peoples, the objective potentiality that challenged man may have differed. It may even be that one man faces different challenges within himself—he may experience the battle of the gods within. But every one of the challenges is as such inescapable and absolute. The challenge cannot be derived from history, since it determines history.

Which objective potentiality, now, is ours? This question turns our attention to the religion that has become our fate, Christianity. But before I speak of Christianity I want to insert a few words on the end of polytheism, and on Buddhism.

The gods of polytheism represent the several great potentialities of man's being. Though they belong together, they are often in conflict among themselves. The internal conflict in which the divine is here engaged, expresses the fact that man, once he has stepped beyond nature, is himself not a peaceful being. He has within him all the conflict pervading nature, and new conflict to boot. In this conflict there are always victors and vanquished. There is no mythology that does not know the night side of life, agony and horror, guilt and death. The ultimate expression of late mythology is Greek tragedy and the Germanic vision of the Twilight of the Gods. This is followed by a form of thought that is no longer specifically mythical. Philosophy arises among the Greeks. I cannot here discuss philosophy. To do it I would have to enter into the question what rational thought really is, and that I cannot attempt in this work. But I shall speak of those religions that now face the night side of life with the full detachment of non-mythical thought: Buddhism and Christianity. To these religions, myth is a form of expression that conceals rather than reveals their essence. That in their historical versions they resemble the mythical religions is due to their misinterpretation by the converts they made among men thinking in mythical terms. Their central concepts on the negative side are, for Buddhism suffering, for Christianity guilt. Their positive concepts cannot be understood without these.

Buddhism reminds us of certain laws we have found earlier, concerning the necessity for the urge to live, and the necessity for the individual's death in the fight for life. All beings want to live, for if the urge to live were not hereditary to them, they would have died out long ago. They kill in order to live, and live in order to die. Life is a never-sated thirst for living and for lust, and creates never-ending suffering. Are these the words of biology or of Buddhism? They are both. They are true. The word of Buddha has been handed down: It is magnificent to behold a creature, terrible to be one.

This doctrine is no longer myth. It is abstract, general thought. It does not accept what the individual says about himself. The individual is wont to bewail his condition, but he hopes for a better one. Life is to him a precious good in spite of everything. Buddhism teaches that this must be so, for without this illusion life could not go on. The will to live would grow confused in its task of self-perpetuation if it were to face the reality of suffering even for a single instant. Existence cannot be without the veil of Maja, and only thought pulls the veil aside.

To describe in a few sentences the Buddhist teaching of salvation from suffering is more than I dare undertake. But I shall attempt to say something about the Christian doctrine of salvation. However, I must at least mention the fact that Buddhism teaches salvation and not despair. Insofar, Buddhism is not pessimism. But it is characteristic of the religions of salvation that they alone make fully visible the despair they overcome. Only as we pass through the abyss does the abyss become part of the past, factual, something we can see clearly. What is alone terrible is to accept nothing but the negative side of these doctrines, and not to join in the step that leads beyond. One can stop at the brink of the abyss, or pass through and beyond it. But one cannot remain in it, and live.

Christianity also speaks of suffering, but it speaks more of guilt. What is guilt? First, guilt is what produces suffering. Guilt is what we do to one another day by day in the fight for life. The individual kills in order to live. But there is more than killing. Theft, envy, calumny, indifference are guilt. Guilt is want of love.

But would not all nature then be guilty? Can I call the lion guilty that slays its prey? The lion would not be a lion if it did not kill. It cannot do otherwise. Can I call guilty the strong man who follows his heroic instincts?

But between lion and man runs the divide of freedom.

The lion has the innocence of nature. Objectively, all nature is in the state which, in man, turns to guilt, but subjectively, nature is not guilty. Man is no longer bound to his instinctive actions. He has insight. The possibility of choice is before him. The man who treats his fellow as the lion treats its prey can do otherwise, and therefore he is guilty.

The story of man's fall expressess this in mythical terms. Man enters into guilt by eating from the tree of knowledge. That tree has been planted by God. "Adam has become like one of us and knows what is good and evil"— this is not only what the serpent had claimed, God Himself says it afterwards. Knowledge is indeed the objective potentiality for which man is meant. Yet by grasping knowledge against the will of God man becomes guilty. Against the will of God, that means against the salutary objective potentiality of knowing. The salutary potentiality of knowing is knowing in love. For man experiences God as love in the redemption from the fall that is revealed in Christ.

Seen with external objectivity, original suffering and original guilt are age-old biological facts. All beings fight the fight for life. All must suffer and die, all must cause suffering and must kill. Subjectively, however, their suffering is less than that of man in proportion to their lesser sensitivity and, above all, their lesser vision of past and future. Man is essentially the suffering being. Man alone bears attributable guilt. But in man's suffering and in his guilt we grow aware of what objectively was there even before. It says in the story of man's fall: "And Adam and Eve saw that they were naked, and they were ashamed." Man is the being who shudders at his own naturalness.

The shudder would be senseless if man did not feel within himself the possibility of a goodness beyond that of instinct, the goodness of insight. And even as the shudder also reflects the desperate external state into which man has fallen by the decay of his instincts, so man's external existence is put in order only through the goodness of insight. One of the ways of ordering is the making of laws. Lawmakers in the olden days were rightly thought to be divine, or divine messengers. For the law orders the life of man by his objective potentiality, by the spirit.

But it turns out that every law that is made is only negative. It bars certain misdeeds, but not the attitude that becomes the source of ever new misdeeds. This is expressed in the Sermon on the Mount. "You have been told: Thou shalt not kill, and he who kills is guilty of judgment. But I say to you, he who is angry with his brother is guilty of judgment. You have been told: Thou shalt not commit adultery. But I say to you, he who looks at a woman to lust after her has already committed adultery with her in his heart." The external regulation of life is not enough. It shifts the guilt to a less visible and hence more dangerous sphere. The stirrings of instinct themselves must be changed.

But even good will cannot accomplish this. This is where the despair that lies in the Christian doctrine of original sin is rooted in experience. I see that I must change my instincts, yet I cannot change them. It has been asked, how can the God of Christianity be a god of love if he gives to his own creatures commandments they cannot keep? Objections of this sort avoid reality and escape into a metaphysical construction. They take at face value in the Christian concept of God what after all is no more than a mythical parable, and neglect that in it which is immediate experience. The conflict exists between two sets of facts both of which can be established objectively: on one hand, the instinct to fight our fellows, an instinct that is there for better or worse; on the other hand, the conditions that have to be met if mankind is to go on living. We can change our faith, but we cannot thereby escape this conflict. The conflict expresses the simple fact that man is a being who cannot remain such as he is. He cannot go back to the innocence of the animal, he must go forward to a new innocence, or perish. And the one possibility open to him, surely, is expressed in the words: God is Love.

What is this love? It is a transformation of man down even into his unconsciousness. It is a fusion of his insight with his instincts, a fusion that makes possible an attitude toward his fellows which was impossible before. The stirrings of man's instincts are the raw material. From this material, love builds a new person. We speak of love even on the level of instincts. Love between man and woman, a mother's love for her child are necessities of human nature. They are strong and beautiful, but at their source they are blind. Christian love is seeing. It is bound up with knowledge, and it is the attitude in which alone knowledge is good. Think of the parable of the good Samaritan. A man lies by the roadside, beaten half to death. Two others pass and do not help him. A third, a stranger, sees *this man needs help,* and helps. Everything is in this seeing. For once the stranger has seen in his heart the other's plight, the help comes almost of itself. Everyone knows full well that he would have to help if he were to see the distress, and looks the other way just for this reason. Love is an attitude of the soul which, in seeing, resolves the fight for life.

Is this love at all possible? Like every true, new possibility, it cannot be derived from what has gone before. Will, of its own power, can perform single good deeds, but it cannot endow itself with love. But once we have experienced the possibility of love, something remains behind in us called conscience. We know then that without love we are missing the essential. Love itself comes from the objective potentiality, from God, and if it comes to us we experience it as an act of grace. Love can be given to us—that is the whole substance of the Christian doctrine of salvation. It is rarely given to us before, in despair of ourselves, we have asked for it.

I could close here. On the level of imperatives, there is nothing for me to add. But it might be said, Christianity has not reformed the world in two thousand years. It may be an ideal, but it does not help us out of our distress. And the reply that the world could have been helped if only it had become truly Christian, that reply would be too cheap. Perhaps it is that the world simply cannot become truly Christian.

Christianity itself, however, is prepared for this its failure in the world. Christ has been crucified. And he has said: "I came to bring not peace but a sword." The sword is the tool of division. He knew he would divide men, not unite them. He foretold his second coming and his kingdom—but only after there had been strife and sorrow, and after his successors had been defeated. What does this mean?

Christian love, to be sure, is a turning toward man such as had not been known before. It intends to be just that. But it creates at the same time a distance between man and his instinct-bound fellow such as had also not been known before. This distance is something Christianity does not intend but cannot avoid. Instinctive love and instinctive hate are bound to their partner with equal blindness. Christian love sees the other human being, and only because of this it is free toward him. But nearly every one of us has a spot where he would much rather be hated blindly than understood clearly. By its mere presence, the love that sees forces a choice upon him whom it sees. This is why it meets with resistance where it cannot arouse love in return.

That resistance is less powerful than the love itself as long as it fights blindly, with the weapons of instinctive nature. In this way Christianity could conquer a large part of the world, though not without surrendering its essence in many respects. But the resistance grows to be a match for Christianity, nay even stronger, when it borrows from Christian love the weapon of knowledge, to wield it with less restraint. Christ renders Anti-Christ possible.

The rationalism of the modern world, though seemingly neutral in this contest, is possible only because of it. I believe that the distance which in the modern mind exists between the subject and the object is a direct legacy of the Christian distance from the world. The true Christian, as an "I," faces the "thou" freely. He sees his fellow and, in this seeing freedom, loves him. When from this attitude love is stricken out while knowledge remains, then fellow-man is no longer approached as a subject. Now everything can be investigated in detached freedom. The subject now looks at an object.

The scientific and technical world of modern man is the result of his daring enterprise, knowledge without love. Such knowledge is in itself neither good nor bad. Its worth depends on what power it serves. Its ideal has been to remain free of any power. Thus it has freed man step by step of all his bonds of instinct and tradition, but has not led him into the new bond of love. The ultimate experience of this freedom from all bonds is what earlier I have called nihilism. When this experience faces its own situation fully, it is perhaps the most honest self-appraisal of the modern world. But just then it is a form of despair. I have said earlier that nihilism seemed to me the negative counterpole of Christianity. It may have become clearer now what I meant. I do believe that the experience of freedom from all bonds, even though it means so far only a question, is closer to love than most other human attitudes that are still bound up with man's instincts. Despair is a question to which the answer comes, at times, from God Himself.

But when knowledge without love becomes the hireling of the resistance against love, then it assumes the role which in the Christian mythical imagery is the role of the devil. The serpent in paradise urges on man knowledge without love. Anti-Christ is the power in history that leads loveless knowledge into the battle of destruction against love. But it is at the same time also the power that destroys itself in its triumph. The battle is still raging. We are in the midst of it, at a post not of our choosing where we must prove ourselves.

I shall say nothing of the future. We do not know the future—rather, we are to act in it. But practical questions I did not mean to treat.

Let me close with the words that Angelus Silesius placed at the end of his *Cherubic Wayfarer:*

> Friend, let this be enough. If thou wouldst go
>   on reading,
> Go and thyself become the writing and the meaning.

Acknowledgments

To chapter i.—The scheme of thinking in the circle of mutual dependence of subject and object was developed by Victor v. Weizsäcker in his *Der Gestaltkreis* (Leipzig, 1940). The concept of the historic character of time was introduced by Bergson; the classic analysis of this concept was given by Heidegger in *Sein und Zeit* (Halle, 1927).

To chapter ii.—Age determination by varved clays originated with De Geer, by intensity of radiation with Milankovitch, by radio-activity probably with Rutherford. Independently of each other, both Holmes and Houtermans, by radio-active methods, have recently arrived at an approximate age of the earth of three billion years (Holmes, *Nature*, 1946; Houtermans, verbal information to the author).

To chapter iv.—The Second Law was found thermodynamically by Carnot and Clausius, its statistical proof was given by Boltzmann. The simile of the Arabs has been much used in the group around Niels Bohr.

To chapter v.—See the more detailed discussion of infinity in my "The World of Physics," to be published shortly by the University of Chicago Press.

To chapter vi.—Pascal Jordan's theory is discussed in his work *Die Herkunft der Sterne* (Stuttgart, 1947).

To chapters x and xi.—See Konrad Lorenz in *Zeitschrift für Tierpsychologie*, V (1942), 235.